T0312298

# Cambridge Elements

### Elements in Global Development Studies
edited by
Peter Ho
*Zhejiang University*
Servaas Storm
*Delft University of Technology*

# MOBILE (FOR) DEVELOPMENT

## *When Digital Giants Take Care of Poor Women*

Marine Al Dahdah
*French National Center for Scientific Research (CNRS), CEMS-IFP*

CAMBRIDGE
UNIVERSITY PRESS

## CAMBRIDGE
### UNIVERSITY PRESS

Shaftesbury Road, Cambridge CB2 8EA, United Kingdom

One Liberty Plaza, 20th Floor, New York, NY 10006, USA

477 Williamstown Road, Port Melbourne, VIC 3207, Australia

314–321, 3rd Floor, Plot 3, Splendor Forum, Jasola District Centre,
New Delhi – 110025, India

103 Penang Road, #05–06/07, Visioncrest Commercial, Singapore 238467

Cambridge University Press is part of Cambridge University Press & Assessment,
a department of the University of Cambridge.

We share the University's mission to contribute to society through the pursuit of
education, learning and research at the highest international levels of excellence.

www.cambridge.org
Information on this title: www.cambridge.org/9781009202428

DOI:10.1017/9781009202398

First published 2022

*A catalogue record for this publication is available from the British Library.*

ISBN 978-1-009-20242-8 Paperback
ISSN 2634-0313 (online)
ISSN 2634-0305 (print)

# Mobile (for) Development

## When Digital Giants Take Care of Poor Women

Elements in Global Development Studies

DOI: 10.1017/9781009202398
First published online: September 2022

Marine Al Dahdah
*French National Center for Scientific Research (CNRS), CEMS-IFP*

**Author for correspondence:** Marine Al Dahdah, marine.aldahdah@ehess.fr

**Abstract:** With their widespread use in the Global South, mobile phones are attracting growing interest from international aid actors and local authorities alike, who are positioning mobile technology as a growth driver and a solution to many social problems. Initiated by giants of the digital industry, these policies are reviving old questions about technological development, the relationship between the market sector and states and the role of technology in the inequalities between the Global North and the Global South. Through a multi-sited ethnography on maternal care in Ghana and India, this Element provides a first-hand look at initiatives that promise to improve poor women's health in the Global South through the use of mobile phones – a field known as Mobile Health, or mHealth. Attentive to the way in which these technical objects modify power relations at both international and local levels, this Element also discusses how mHealth transforms care practices and healthcare.

This Element also has a video abstract: www.cambridge.org/Al_Dahdah

**Keywords:** mHealth, mobile technology, maternal health, India, Ghana

ISBNs: 9781009202428 (PB), 9781009202398 (OC)
ISSNs: 2634-0313 (online), 2634-0305 (print)

# Contents

## Introduction

Propelled by new philanthropists, mHealth programmes recreate old paths of dependency and contribute to the influence of the North American and European digital industry by creating new markets in the Global South. By focusing on individual solutions to address structural issues, these initiatives displace and reinforce multiple inequalities. Indeed, mobile technology introduces technical and commercial criteria that condition access to healthcare, thus transforming mechanisms of inclusion and exclusion of individuals. This Element focuses on the way in which these technical objects modify power relations at both international and local levels. It invites us to examine how mobile technology is contributing to the emergence of new forms of power, to the reconfiguration of social roles, to the globalisation of devices, to the datafication of health and to the transformation of healthcare and health practices.

The Element uses the case study of the Mobile Technology for Community Health (Motech) mobile platform – today one of the most widely used in the Global South – to analyse the particular ways in which this mobile health technology sets out to influence and organise others, as well as the discourses of promise or fear mobilised to achieve these goals. Through a multi-sited ethnography of Motech in Ghana and India, this Element provides a first-hand look at initiatives that promise to improve health in the Global South through the use of mobile phones. From the Gates Foundation offices to community health centres in the villages of India and Ghana, this investigation clarifies the sociotechnical assemblages and datafication processes specific to mHealth in a globalised biomedical field and analyses the consequences of mobile technologies on the delivery of care and on the health of the women enrolled in the Motech programme.

The Motech case study shows how, with targeted funding, influential players are defining the mobile phone as a relevant solution to meet development and health challenges. This Element discusses the way mHealth intervenes in care practices, and questions its role in recent transformations of healthcare and administration aimed at reducing expenses and optimising resources. The Element examines the forms of healthcare management, outsourcing and empowerment proposed by Motech, which reflect a determination to use mobile technology as a means of delegating care to responsible patients and digital healthcare workers. It shows that mHealth devices that seek to substitute digitised information for hands-on healthcare practice meet with strong resistance in the field, and result in deterioration of care and of the healthcare system in general. mHealth technologies have significant implications for social inequalities: this Element studies the gender relations at work in Motech and the way in which the device proposes new reassignments by positioning the mobile phone as a means of empowerment and a way of compensating for gender inequalities. It shows, through comparative analysis, how this mHealth programme confirms, amplifies or mitigates forms of domination and inequality. The Element combines the analysis of technical devices proposed by science and technology studies (STS) with a sociological analysis of health inequalities, showing that while mobile tools may be conditioned by unequal relationships, their presence and the ways in which they are used alter these relationships in return.

## 1 Mobile Health: A 'Simply Brilliant' Innovation

This introductory section explores the origins and growth of mobile technologies in health and development. Information and communication technologies (ICTs) only represent one of the most recent sets of technologies in an already long history of innovations, tools and strategies for development.[1] At the same time, ICTs, with the mobile phone as their flagship, tend to take so much importance in development policies that one could frame the last decade as the period during which a 'digital turn' took place in development policies (Al Dahdah and Quet, 2020). mHealth programmes also align with new international public health standards described as 'global health' (Adams, Novotny and Leslie, 2008; Gaudillière *et al.*, 2020); they are utilised by global players, respond to global challenges, mobilise surveillance and quantification technologies and engage strong participation by private actors. Indeed, the dynamics of globalisation and commodification associated with global health encourage the spread of technical devices such as mHealth in the Global South (Al Dahdah, 2019a; Sawadogo *et al.*, 2021). The innovative and transformative component of mHealth constitutes a central argument to promote its spreading in the developing world. This first section sets out the 'promising communication' rationale in mHealth discourses, which contributes to the promotion of the mobile phone as a 'simply brilliant' innovation for health.[2] Indeed, for its

---

[1] ICTs have been associated with promises of development for a long time. For instance, the Okinawa Charter in 2001 or the Millenium Development Goals in 2000 already gave ICTs an important role. Not to mention the longer tradition of mass media communication for development in the 1960s and 1970s.

[2] This section is based on a qualitative discourse analysis of four textual corpora compiled using Factiva software. The first Factiva corpus, called 'Worldwide General Press', comprised 446 articles published between 2011 and 2013, in English and French, with 'mobile AND health' as the key topic. The second Factiva corpus, 'Techno and Health Specialized Press', focused only on the four most mentioned regions in the general press (Africa, India, the United Kingdom and the United States) and comprised 581 articles published between 2011 and 2013 in the specialist technical and health press, with 'mobile AND health' as the key topic. The third corpus,

promoters mHealth is much more than just a phone (Section 1.1) or just healthcare (Section 1.2). From 2010 onwards, the private sector has been investing substantial sums in mHealth projects to improve women's health, and several international initiatives have proposed using mobile phones to accelerate improvements in maternal health (Section 1.3). The field of maternal health is therefore particularly relevant to explore the development of mHealth and the associated public health transformations.

> 'Using mobile phones to access and relay health information in developing countries is the topic everyone in health and technology is talking about right now. There's a reason for that, of course. It's one of those 'simply brilliant' innovations that seems to make perfect sense'.
> (Bill & Melinda Gates Foundation blog, published on 3 October 2011)

Access to mobile phones is becoming increasingly common worldwide, and is driving access to the internet, especially in the developing world (ITU, 2019). Mobile health projects and applications emerged at the beginning of the 2000s, and have mushroomed in developing countries over the last decade (Chib, van Velthoven and Car, 2015). Aware of the increasing deployment of mobile technology, international health actors have sought to characterise this phenomenon more precisely. In 2011, the World Health Organization (WHO) first defined mHealth as the practice of medicine and public health assisted by mobile technologies, such as mobile phones, patient-monitoring devices, 'personal digital assistants' and other wireless technologies (WHO, 2011).

The WHO segments mHealth according to a typology of projects that include the following:

1. Communication from individuals to health services (call centres, helplines or hotlines)
2. Communication from health services to individuals (appointment or treatment reminders, awareness and mobilisation campaigns on health issues)
3. Communication between health professionals (mobile telemedicine, patient monitoring, diagnostic and decision aids).

---

'Scientific Press', was compiled using PubMed; it comprised 213 articles published between 2010 and 2014, with 'mobile AND health' as the key topic. The fourth corpus, 'International Reports', comprised some twenty reports from international and UN agencies (UN, EU, World Bank, WHO, UNDP, ITU, UNICEF, OECD, US FDA, Indian Government, Institute for Healthcare Informatics) published between 2010 and 2014 on information and communication technologies (ICTs) for development or on mHealth, as well as fifty reports from the GSM Association and twenty from the mHealth Alliance, the two major international organisations that promote mHealth worldwide. I have already published a detailed analysis on these promises in two articles 'Mobile health and maternal care: a winning combination for healthcare in the developing world?' M Al Dahdah *et al.*, (2015) and 'mHealth: The ubiquitous source of health information?' M Al Dahdah *Le Temps des medias*, 52–65,2014.

Today, mHealth figures come mainly from mobile operators and mobile technology providers. They estimate the size of the global mHealth market at USD 45.7 billion in 2020 and expect it to grow at a compound annual growth rate of 17.6 per cent from 2021 to 2028,[3] a rather approximate estimate that focuses mostly on applications and services that are accessible in rich countries.[4] Most of these services are smartphone-based and thus currently still beyond the reach of much of the developing world. Consequently, most of the projects deployed in resource-poor settings over the past decade have been SMS-based or voice services, which can be used on a classic handset. Even with a relatively low-tech profile, the innovative and transformative component of mHealth constitutes a central argument for promoting its spread in the developing world: '*Mobile phones and wireless internet end isolation, and will therefore prove to be the most transformative technology of economic development of our time*' (Jeffrey Sachs, 2008 quoted in World Bank, 2012, 1). Such call for technological change and the futures and promises it conveys are structuring the field of mHealth for developing countries. Indeed, for its advocates, mHealth is much more than just a phone or just healthcare.

## 1.1 More Than Just a Phone

STS scholars have already identified these dynamics as characteristic of many innovative devices. In line with the work of Pierre-Benoît Joly on the economy of technoscientific promises, or Patrice Flichy on imaginaries of innovation or Kaushik Sunder Rajan on promises as a symptom of technoscientific capitalism (Flichy, 2003; Joly, Rip and Callon, 2013; Rajan, 2012), my analysis points to a clear form of 'promise-based communication' at play in discourses around mHealth (Quet, 2012). All these promises help to promote the mobile phone as a 'simply brilliant' innovation for health. Some of them – unrelated to health – are fed by the general hopes and hypes associated with the mobile phone. According to mHealth promoters, the ubiquity and accessibility of mobile phones allow everybody to be easily connected with anybody, anywhere, at any time, making this technology both omnipotent and universal. Moreover, according to several UN agencies and international organisations, mobile phones are central to the economic growth of developing countries: '[*increased mobile ownership is*] *likely to have twice as large an impact on economic*

---

[3] See for example: *mHealth Market Size, Share & Trends Report:* www.grandviewresearch.com/industry-analysis/mhealth-market

[4] See for example: research2guidance. « mHealth App Economics 2017 », novembre 2017. https://research2guidance.com/wp-content/uploads/2017/10/1-mHealth-Status-And-Trends-Reports.pdf. Pew Research Center. « Mobile Health 2012 », november 2012. www.pewinternet.org/2012/11/08/mobile-health-2012/.

*growth in developing countries as in developed ones because the starting point of infrastructure in poorer countries is so much lower in terms of landlines and broadband access*' (UNDP, 2012, 10). These devices also serve as substitutes for many useful tools that are rarely found in the poorest countries, such as cameras, debit cards or voice recorders (World Bank, 2012, 4). Coming on top of such 'mobile promises', promises about healthcare further inflate the general tendency of these discourses to keep on promising.

## 1.2 More Than Just Healthcare

The use of mobile and wireless technologies to support the achievement of health objectives (mHealth) has the potential to transform the face of health service delivery across the globe. *(WHO, 2011, 9)*

Mobile applications can lower costs and improve the quality of healthcare as well as shift behaviour to strengthen prevention, all of which can improve health outcomes over the long term. *(World Bank, 2011, 9)*

Three major promises – effectiveness, cost-efficiency and empowerment – are constantly used to promote mHealth as a transformative healthcare device. These three promises are foundational to mHealth. They give content and credit to this new field, but also raise expectations that may not be fulfilled, or inspire dreams that may not come true. The effectiveness of healthcare and efficiency of health workers are improved, it is suggested, by using mobile and digital health data. Instantly updated data, collected onsite, facilitates emergency and crisis management (Callaway *et al.,* 2012; Case, Morrison and Vuylsteke, 2012; Massey and Gao, 2010). Mobile apps are reported to improve the quality and accuracy of diagnosis by compiling 'good practices', disseminating international protocols, analysing personal health records and offering personalised treatments in accordance with these indicators (Alepis and Lambrinidis, 2013; Yu, Li and Liu, 2013). mHealth can reach the patient wherever he or she is, even if there are no health facilities in the vicinity. In developed countries, isolated patients can call and exchange health data directly with health professionals through mobile apps (Sankaranarayanan and Sallach, 2013). This new connectivity can emerge even without widespread mobile phone ownership, through community health workers (CHWs) sent to isolated communities to collect health data on their mobiles, evaluate needs and connect the local populations instantly to health facilities (Källander *et al.,* 2013; Mahmud, Rodriguez and Nesbit, 2010).

Moreover, mHealth is also presented as a low-cost means of rationalising health expenses and even as a way of streamlining health expenditure.

According to its promoters, mHealth reduces health costs by optimising medical time, by avoiding unnecessary hospitalisations, redundant exams or superfluous medicines, and by preventing missed appointments or interruption of treatment. Furthermore, when combined with mBanking, mHealth ensures security of out-of-pocket payments even for patients without bank accounts, and enables uninsured patients to apply for micro-insurance schemes to cover their health expenses (mHealth Alliance and World Economic Forum, 2011; mHealth Alliance, 2012; World Bank, 2012).

Finally, the promise of 'empowerment' is crucial as it is the only 'human' or 'patient-centred' justification for these devices: the only one focused on the individual and not only on the optimisation of healthcare services. Far from its original meaning of a grassroots acquisition or reinforcement of power, 'empowerment' in the case of mHealth largely boils down to giving patients a limited degree of autonomy and accountability. This promise echoes the individualistic and liberal vision of empowerment adopted by international aid agencies at the beginning of 2000 and critiqued by several scholars (Calvès, 2009; Parpart *et al.*, 2003; Sardenberg, 2008). The empowering effect of mHealth serves to justify the idea of increased patient autonomy with regard to the healthcare system, and also the vision of shared accountability. Health cannot be fully delegated to health professionals; patients have to shoulder their share of responsibility too. For mHealth advocates, mobile phones play a key role in this empowerment through the optimisation of prevention and treatments. Firstly, easy access to health information via mobile devices will lead to healthy behaviours. By improving the understanding of preventive actions, risky behaviours will be avoided and healthier ones adopted. These 'positive health-seeking behaviours' will in the long run improve the health of whole populations. Secondly, a better understanding of treatments will improve compliance with medical instructions and prescriptions. Studies have already been conducted on treatment adherence for chronic diseases in Western countries to show that alerts, reminders and follow-ups sent by mobile phones help patients to follow instructions and treatments (Cocosila and Archer, 2005; Lester *et al.*, 2010; Stoner and Hendershot, 2012), thus 'empowered chronic patients' no longer need to visit the health facility so often and are more in charge of their own health. Closer to a liberal than a liberating vision of empowerment, the technological empowerment of mHealth maximises individual interest and should thereby ensure efficient healthcare delivery. Maternal mHealth projects deployed in the developing world provide telling illustrations of this techno-liberal vision of empowerment (Al Dahdah, 2019b).

## 1.3 Maternal Health, a Productive Sector for mHhealth

Half a million women die every year worldwide as a result of pregnancy or childbirth, almost all (99 per cent) in developing countries. Millions of women experience pregnancy-related morbidity, sometimes with severe consequences that could be avoided through better information and better monitoring of expectant mothers (WHO *et al.*, 2012). Clinicians report that late arrival at a health facility is the main cause of death for women in labour. Among the multiple reasons for this delayed care are distance, lack of transport, poor quality of primary healthcare services, poverty, lack of information or education and women's social status (Ronsmans and Graham, 2006). Large disparities remain worldwide in terms of prenatal care coverage and skilled attendance during childbirth. Poor women living in remote areas are less likely to receive adequate care. This is especially true in areas where the number of qualified health workers is low, especially in sub-Saharan Africa, Southeast Asia and Oceania. Improving maternal health has been one of the Millennium Development Goals set by the United Nations (MDG5) for the past two decades and is now part of Sustainable Development Goal 3. The objective of reducing maternal mortality rates by three quarters between 1990 and 2015 proved difficult to attain, and some actors have sought new dynamics to meet this target. Since 2010, the private sector (mobile operators, pharmaceutical firms, philanthropic foundations, etc.) has invested massively in 'mHealth' projects involving the use of mobile technologies to improve women's health, and several international initiatives have advocated using mobile phones to make up ground in addressing maternal health issues (mHealth Alliance and UN Foundation, 2013; Weil *et al.*, 2013).

The field of maternal health is therefore particularly relevant for exploring the development of mHealth and the associated public health transformations (institutional overhaul, transnationalisation, the increasing role of communication technologies, gender relationships and expertise), but has not been widely researched to date. The available articles on the subject consist of literature reviews of existing projects (Noordam *et al.*, 2011; Tamrat and Kachnowski, 2011), or reports on the use of mobile phones by a group of midwives in Northern Indonesia (Chib, 2010) and in Thai border areas (Kaewkungwal *et al.*, 2010) or the use of persuasive messages addressed to women in rural India (Ramachandran and Goswami, 2010). The rapid development of mobile health projects addressing maternal health can be explained in part by the supposedly widespread access to mobile phones by women; gender differences in accessing new technologies are much smaller when it comes to mobile phone access.

Several gender studies have shown that access to ICT is (or has long been, in developed countries) generally more difficult for women, who are less well equipped – the computer, for example, remains the property of the husband – and therefore less accustomed to ICT (Wyatt, 2005). The presence and dominant position of males in the construction of ICT technologies may also explain why women struggle to find their place in these same technologies (Gurumurthy, 2004; Henwood and Wyatt, 2000). Sociology – and feminist sociology in particular – has provided ample insights into the distribution of social roles within ICT, gender inequalities in professional practices, the impact of ICT on socialisation (or indeed on the dissolution of social bonds) and its dominance effects (Gardey, 2003; Haraway *et al.*, 2007). Certain studies have focused specifically on internet applications (Suchman, 2008; Wajcman, 2000). Mobile phones, however, hold a special place in the world of ICT: women are 21 per cent less likely than men to own a mobile phone; gender differences do exist, therefore, but mobile phones are a more 'egalitarian technology' than the computer or internet because their cost is lower and they require little training to operate (GSMA, 2013).

This Element contributes to an understanding of gender relations in the context of mobile tools developed specifically for women's health. It offers to study both how mobile technologies shape 'gendered' relationships and how gender relationships have an impact on the actual construction of technological projects, a point that will be studied in depth in Section 6. This research draws on a wide literature combining Science, Technology and Society studies and Information and Communication Sciences to reveal the transformations, power issues and inequalities at work in these new sociotechnical artefacts. It is based on empirical data collected between 2014 and 2019 in Ghana and India and focuses particularly on the case study of Motech. A brief overview of the concepts and methods employed for this research project is required here in order to understand how mHealth is deployed in development contexts.

## 2 Key Concepts and Methods for Studying mHealth

This section describes how this research approaches mHealth as a new object of study in the social sciences, describing the disciplinary and methodological frameworks as well as the material and logistical contingencies of fieldwork that both enabled and conditioned this work. It describes the precise form of the object of study: the Motech health initiative rolled out in Ghana and in India, detailing the approach, the method, the fieldwork areas and the tools adopted in order to study it. This research is interdisciplinary, combining approaches from the sociology and anthropology of science, technology and health, the sociology of usage and media and discourse analysis.

## 2.1 STS, Usage and Discourse Analysis

This work adopts three main theoretical orientations. The first approach is that of 'Science, Technology and Society' studies, which analyses the intertwining of the social and the technical within scientific or technological systems and artefacts. The studies of artefacts undertaken in the context of techno-social innovation (Bijker and Law, 1992; MacKenzie and Wajcman, 1999) and Actor-Network Theory, which identifies the sociotechnical networks that lie at the heart of the construction of technical objects (Akrich *et al.*, 2006), are key references. The analysis of science and technology in the biomedical field (Akrich and Méadel, 2007, 2010; Cassier, 2002; Epstein, 2007; Gaudillière, 2002) and key STS concepts applied to the countries of the South and to the context of globalisation (Anderson, 2009; Arvanitis *et al.*, 2008; de Laet and Mol, 2000; Shrum, 2000) are of particular importance for this research and are fully mobilised in Section 3 on global dependencies and Section 4 on datafication.

The second approach, which can be seen as an STS subfield, is that of the study of ICT usage, focusing on how communication technologies in practice impact women's health and healthcare. This field lies at the crossroads between the analysis of media communication, the social history of technology and the sociology of lifestyles. The observation of usage, that is what people actually do with these technical objects and devices, is a useful methodological entry point for understanding the impact of mHealth projects. The impact of objects on the social has been studied methodically by several colleagues (Conein, Dodier and Thévenot, 1993; Jouët, 2000; Proulx, 2005). The analysis proposed here is not restricted to innovative digital uses that concern a limited population of privileged women; it also addresses established uses of these technologies (Edgerton, 1998) as well as identifying non-users of the technologies and the reasons for their non-use (Wyatt, 2010). Both health workers and patients are users of mHealth programmes; the uses and impacts of such technologies are illustrated mainly in Section 5 on health worker performance and Section 6 on the technological inequalities faced by targeted patients. In Section 6, I also develop a gendered approach to mobile usage, as the patients targeted in the studied programme are pregnant women.

Finally, I propose to enrich the study of ICT usage with an analysis of the associated discourses, by building up a corpus of relevant texts produced on and by the devices under study, reflecting the various competing discourses (media, institutional, commercial, advertising, legal, financial, technical, etc.). This qualitative and quantitative discourse analysis is further enriched by its juxtaposition with user perceptions. The cross-comparison of usage studies with discourse analysis is a key element in the framing of this research. This threefold 'STS-usage-discourse' approach articulates the study of usage with sociopolitical and discursive approaches to shed light on the power issues that underlie how the uses of a technology develop in a particular social context.

## 2.2 Multi-Sited Investigation: Grasping the Dynamics and Anchorage Points of a 'Global' Object

This Element proposes to approach mobile health as a 'global assemblage', that is as a global form of technoscience that articulates technological, political and ethical questions within a single artefact (Ong and Collier, 2005). How can we write an ethnography of a global object? How can concrete, empirical practices and experiences help us to better understand processes that are by definition diffuse and composite? Following on from the work of Anna Tsing (Tsing, 2005), this research looks at how 'global forces' articulate with local sites. The idea is not to superimpose the 'global' on the 'local', any more than it is to compile a 'global' portrait by piecing together empirically observed 'local' particularities. Hitherto, studies of mHealth have typically been limited to a single geographic space of observation and a single mHealth application. However, multi-sited or transnational research into this topic seems relevant for several reasons. Multi-sited analysis – which emphasises fieldwork in multiple and heterogeneous spaces and was advocated by the anthropologist George Marcus (Marcus, 1995) before being taken up by numerous scholars (Fassin, 2006; Fischer, 2003; Jasanoff, 2005; Rajan, 2008) – is especially conducive to the study of ICT in a globalised context. This analysis meets the new methodological requirements for the study of contemporary social reconfigurations; this type of inquiry is also well suited to the study of moving objects such as the universal symbol of mobility, the mobile phone.

The aim is not simply to compare two similar objects of research but to trace links, juxtapositions and connections between different objects and places. It is also to track the movements and developments of the people, objects, ideas, symbols, signs, tensions and conflicts embedded in these various projects, and this can only be done by diversifying the areas of fieldwork. mHealth raises international issues: its financing, technical implementation, infrastructures and fields of application are managed by different actors located around the globe. The underlying transnational mechanisms of these different applications can be brought to light only through an analysis that involves varied cultural areas and different socio-economic contexts. mHealth is not a finished product; no picture of the phenomenon could ever be complete. In a very concrete way, multi-sited research takes the form of chains and paths along which the sites are juxtaposed, and the goal is to identify their links, connections and nodes. I elected to study multiple mHealth sites, that is several mobile phone-based health initiatives, tracing their connections and identifying the nodes that link them together. The starting point for this analysis is the sociotechnical device that constitutes the local mHealth implementation 'site'. Mobile Midwife in Ghana is one such mHealth site, Kilkari in Bihar is another; the study of these sites, their links and their connections, is the core of my research, enabling me to analyse global health forces as they relate to these sites. The methodology used for this research combines participant observation with sociological interviews of actors selected by purposive sampling (women, health workers, physicians, financial and technical partners and representatives of the various organisations that sponsor or are associated with the projects, such as governments, access providers, etc.) and with the compilation and analysis of a corpus of texts in English, published on the web and in the press, covering the different mHealth projects studied. Each field study involves three lines of inquiry: a biography of the project, a study of the uses of the device and an analysis of the discourses around the project.

## 2.3 Studying the 'Most Promising mHealth Project'

In the least developed countries (LDCs), only 19 per cent of individuals were online in 2019 (latest figures). Sub-Saharan Africa and South Asia have in common the highest proportions of non-internet users as well as the highest mobile phone and mobile internet growth rates worldwide, twice the rate of the rest of the world (ITU, 2013, 2014, 2019). These two regions are also those with the world's shortest healthy life expectancy at birth, the highest infant and maternal mortality rates and the worst indicators of the United Nations millennium development goals (UNICEF, World Bank and WHO, 2013; WHO, 2013). The idea that the growing phenomenon of mobile phones could lead to a better health situation for Africans and South Asians emerged and took shape in an increasingly number of mHealth projects in these two regions. To better understand this phenomenon, I conducted multiple fieldworks in both regions between 2014 and 2019, studying several mHealth projects – among them the 'most promising mHealth project':

> The most promising mHealth project that I have seen, called Motech, focuses on maternal and child health in Ghana. Community health workers with phones visit villages and submit digital forms with vital information about newly pregnant women. The system then sends health messages to the

expectant mothers, such as weekly reminders about good pre-natal care. The system also sends data to the health ministry, giving policymakers an accurate and detailed picture of health conditions in the country. Those working on AIDS, tuberculosis, malaria, family planning, nutrition, and other global health issues can use the same platform, so that all parts of a country's health system are sharing information and responding appropriately in real-time. This is the dream, but it works only if frontline workers are inputting data, health ministries are acting on it, and patients are using the information that they receive on their phones.

(Bill Gates in 'The Optimist's Timeline' 31.12.2012 on livemint.com)

The Motech project was launched in 2010 in Ghana by the Grameen Foundation with the financial support of the Bill & Melinda Gates Foundation (BMGF). The goal of Motech is to improve maternal, newborn and child health outcomes in rural developing contexts by supporting women during their pregnancy and newborns during their first year of life. The project combines health information modules for women and health professionals with identification and tracking of patients, collection and processing of health data, and the use of SMS alerts and voice messages. The aim of Motech is to become a global platform used worldwide for different health issues, to sustain and increase the quality and accessibility of health information and care. The Motech project was subsequently launched in India (Bihar state) in 2012, building on the Ghanaian experience. Motech relies exclusively on the community level of the healthcare system to function. In Ghana, the community health system relies on Community Health Nurses trained by the Ministry of Health (Ntsua *et al.*, 2012). In India, community health is a two-pillar system: Anganwadi Workers (AWWs) are appointed by the 'Ministry of Women and Child Development', whereas Accredited Social Health Activists (ASHAs) are overseen by the 'Ministry of Health'. Both types of CHWs are the key cadre in India's CHW programmes designed to improve maternal and child health (Al Dahdah and Kumar, 2021). Section 5 is dedicated to the particular role attributed to CHWs in Motech's deployment.

In Ghana, the Motech project began in 2010 and finished at the end of 2014, before being 'transferred' to the major mobile operator, MTN. In August 2014, it was active in 7 of the approximately 200 districts of Ghana. About 30,000 women had been registered since 2010, including 9,000 in Gomoa, in the Central region, where I conducted my fieldwork. The project studied the implementation of two interrelated services using mobile phones: Mobile Midwife, a health information messaging service for pregnant women and lactating mothers, and the Nurse Application, a client data management system for CHWs (Grameen Foundation, 2012; Figure 1). The aim of Mobile Midwife

**Figure 1** Mobile midwife ad

is to provide maternal health information for pregnant women, mothers with children under twelve months and their families. Women can sign up for the free mobile phone-based service, which sends text or voice messages in one of the multiple regional languages with time-specific health information. The weekly messages encourage pregnant women to seek antenatal and postnatal care. The messages continue throughout the child's first year, with health information for mothers and children, such as family planning and immunisation alerts.

Kilkari is the Indian version of Mobile Midwife. Launched in Bihar in 2013, it is part of a bigger project called Ananya, which encompasses three mHealth applications. Initially launched in eight districts of Bihar, it was subsequently extended to twenty districts, reaching 100,000 subscribers in the first two years. Fieldwork was conducted in two of the eight pilot districts with the highest rates of subscription to Kilkari. Kilkari is the only mobile application in the Ananya programme that is directly aimed at pregnant women. Like Mobile Midwife in Ghana, Kilkari is a voice messaging system that provides maternal health information for pregnant women and mothers with children aged under twelve months (Figure 2). Running on the same Motech platform, the weekly messages advise women on how to pursue their pregnancy, and also encourage them to seek antenatal and postnatal care. It is a fee-based mobile phone service, sending time-specific voice messages in 'rural Hindi', at a cost of 1 rupee per message. Complementary to Kilkari, Mobile Kunji is a set of illustrated cards issued to CHWs, containing shortcodes that they can dial on their mobile

**Figure 2** Kilkari ad

phones in order to get pregnant women to listen to the same Kilkari health messages (Figure 3). Whereas Mobile Kunji will never be extended outside Bihar, Kilkari was selected for nationwide roll-out.

### THE MOTECH FIELDWORK

In 2014–2015, I conducted an empirical qualitative study in Ghana (Central Region) and in India (Bihar state), where the Motech project was deployed. In Ghana, I went with a research team from the School of Public Health (University of Ghana) to Central Ghana – the region with highest rate of enrolment to Motech – 10 focus groups of women were organised in 2 districts, where we met 100 women. We also interviewed twenty health workers involved in the mHealth programme, and fifteen implementers. In Bihar, I went with a research assistant to two of the eight pilot districts of the project, choosing the two districts where the subscriptions rates to the service where the highest. We met twenty implementers of Motech in Delhi, and in the two selected districts, we met the managers of community health centres, who connected us with the CHWs. We then

**Figure 3** Mobile Kunji cards
**Source:** BBC Media Action (India): www.rethink1000days.org

organised focus groups with CHWs involved in the service and, thanks to them, held focus groups with women in thirteen villages. I met a total of ninety-nine women and thirty CHWs in Bihar. All interviews were conducted in local languages (Fanté in Ghana and Hindi in Bihar) and were fully transcribed into English and imported into nVivo software, along with the field notes, for qualitative analysis. I used a two-step coding method: a first round of descriptive thematic coding followed by a second round of analytic coding related to my research questions.

After presenting the research object of this Element, the concepts and methods that guided this investigation, the following four sections will each be dedicated to one major finding. Section 3 focuses on global dependencies in the design and implementation of mHealth programmes and Motech. It shows how mHealth demonstrates a new convergence of development policies with the interests of technology providers. Section 4 explores the importance of data collection and data work in mHealth and their use for healthcare purposes. Mobile telephony plays an important role in the 'datafication' of developing countries as it represents, in many development contexts, the sole and unique instrument of digital quantification. This section sets out to study how the digital data generated by mHealth in the Global South is collected, protected and used. Section 5 discusses the way mHealth intervenes in care practices and questions its role in recent transformations of care and its administration aimed at reducing expenses and optimising health resources. It highlights the drifts of a 'datafication' of health used for managerial monitoring purposes, where clinical activities are evaluated using traces of mobile application usage. Section 6 studies the gender relations at work in Motech and the way in which the device proposes new responsibilities by positioning the mobile phone as a means for empowerment and of compensating for gender inequalities. However, the analysis goes beyond this observation and shows through comparative analysis how the mHealth programme confirms, amplifies or mitigates domination and inequality.

## 3 Global Dependencies and North–South Inequalities

mHealth demonstrates a new convergence between development policies and the interests of telecoms and digital players. Previously little involved in the field of international health, mobile phone operators (including Vodafone, Airtel and Orange), digital manufacturers (Intel, Microsoft, Voxiva and Facebook) and their foundations are becoming key players in these health programmes. Funded and implemented by the Gates, Grameen and BBC Foundations in partnership with the Ministries of Health of Ghana and India, Motech is an emblematic example of this convergence and serves to document the inequalities that characterise this type of public–private partnership (PPP). The BMGF was Motech's main sponsor from its launch in Ghana in 2010 to the nationwide extension of the project in India in 2016. The Motech project is based on three PPPs: firstly, between the Gates Foundation and the Ghanaian Ministry of Health (Ghana Health Service (GHS)); secondly, between the Gates Foundation and the State of Bihar; and thirdly, between the Gates Foundation and the Central (i.e. national) Ministry of Health in India. The other transversal actor of the project, the Grameen Foundation, is in charge of the technical part of the programme and also its implementation in Ghana. The implementation of Motech in Bihar is managed by BBC Media Action (the private foundation of the British Broadcasting Corporation). The Gates Foundation is Motech's main actor and funder; it forms different partnerships depending on project configurations and deployment sites. Here I present the stakeholders who visibly participated in Motech. These designers and project managers work with a multitude of local operators involved in the initiatives, but the role of these local operators – and sometimes even the identity of their employer (often an NGO or a local company) – is hidden, as they are frequently presented as employees of one of the three private foundations (BMGF, Grameen or BBC), but they are actually subcontractors (Al Dahdah, 2019a).

Who owns the technologies proposed by these development programmes? Are the beneficiary countries of the Global South able to modify their form and content? Can they maintain the programme themselves without outside help? The experience of Motech provides an answer to these questions, and a more precise understanding of where North–South inequalities come into play when mobile devices for development are deployed in the Global South. This section draws on the history of science and technology while remaining mindful of the historical continuities between different power regimes that utilise science and technology for the purposes of domination (Petitjean, Jami and Moulin, 1992). This awareness situates current forms of domination within a continuity, showing that the regime of domination at work in the programmes studied in Ghana and India, though dressed in new clothes, relies on ancient patterns of exploitation and subservience (Arnold, 2000; Brukum, 1985). In what follows, I will be exploring four areas in which the North–South inequalities associated with mobile platforms are enacted: knowledge and knowhow; ownership issues; systems interoperability; and the cost of the programmes.

## 3.1 Blaming the Technical Skills Deficit

Developing and managing information systems calls for specialised knowledge and specific knowhow, but digital development actors consider that the countries where these technical initiatives are deployed do not possess this knowledge and so cannot manage and maintain the systems without help from the 'developed' countries. Motech provides an excellent illustration of this belief, which maintains an inequality of knowledge between North and South.

When the GHS collaborates in telehealth projects, two of its departments – the Directorate of Policy Planning, Monitoring and Evaluation and the Directorate of Information and Communication – are particularly concerned. The first was involved from the conception of the Motech project in 2010 for logistical reasons, as it oversees the health structures and personnel indispensable to the ground-level deployment of the Motech system. Nevertheless, this crucial role played by the GHS is no longer in evidence when one examines the technical side of the system. The GHS does not own the Motech technical platform, has no access to the database that is enriched by its own teams and cannot use Motech without an agreement with the Grameen Foundation, which manages the platform. If the ministry has been kept at arm's length for the technical part of Motech, it is, according to certain actors, due to a lack of 'technical skills'. The Grameen Foundation casts doubt on the ministry's capacity to administer the Motech platform, positioning itself as the only technical operator able to manage Motech. During the field investigation in Ghana, however, several professionals from outside the ministry and outside Grameen who had worked for Motech suggested that if the ministry's

Information and Communication Directorate had been integrated into the project, it would have had the skills to manage the Motech platform.

By excluding the ministry's technicians, the Grameen Foundation does not offer Ghanaian engineers the opportunity to acquire the knowhow associated with this specific platform and does not draw on their ground-level knowledge. During the fieldwork I met with both of the ministry directorates and attended training sessions on mHealth applications developed by the Information and Communication Directorate. While the ministry teams may not master the exact same code as Motech, they nonetheless develop and administer similar mobile health information systems and could therefore learn to use the Motech code so as to manage this platform in addition to the others. The Indian case is comparable. Even though India ranks as a giant in digital technology, the Indian ministry does not manage the Motech platform. As the ministry officials explained to me, the specificities of the servers required mean that the American Foundations must retain control over Motech.

This judgement about the aptitude of the countries of the South to manage information systems is an omnipresent feature of digital development projects. It points to a major inequality between the project managers and the recipients of these programmes, reflecting a desire to box in the technical object by proposing configurations that are too specific to be managed locally and adapted to local configurations. As Robert Wade explains, these technological programmes enclose the countries of the South in a new dependence on the North by relying on technological standards and regimes developed by and for the Global North (Wade, 2002). The technical capabilities of the countries of the South are indeed an important challenge for the long-term incorporation of these technical systems. However, in the case of Motech, it was for other reasons that the transfer of skills did not take place, since in 2013 Ghana, like India, had the human and technological resources to manage a platform such as Motech. The study of Motech reveals problems around platform ownership, interoperability and significant costs, which played a still larger role than the 'technical capabilities' of the South in the way the system was deployed.

## 3.2 Closing Down 'Open-Source' Devices

The Motech 'platform' – or 'suite', as it is called by its designers – refers to the IT system that brings together the programmes required to operate the applications that drive Motech Ghana and Motech India. Questions around the ownership and rights of use in the Motech platform are met with contrasting responses. According to the Grameen Foundation, the question of ownership rights does not arise, as Motech is a platform with an open-source (and therefore free access) licence, as one Grameen employee explains: '*If you want to use Motech, it's open source, you just go on the internet, you download it and look at the code and see what it does, if you need any help then you come to us*'. For the Ghanaian Health Ministry, however, the Grameen Foundation is the sole owner of the platform, as they told me: '*The Motech platform is owned by the Grameen Foundation. The data belongs to the Grameen Foundation right now and the platform is used by them for other countries such as India*'. The open-source licence is accessible to all: there is no need to pay for ownership rights in order to use the platform, but it is necessary to acquire essential technical skills and knowledge in order to use the html code, and to configure and operate all of the Motech components.

While open source is often held up as a tool that compensates for unequal access to software, it remains a technical artefact that is difficult to transfer (Sim and Philip, 2008). There is no 'owner' of Motech with established copyright, but in practice only the Grameen Foundation can use the platform. The two other Ghanaian mHealth applications – No Yawa and CCH – that used Motech in 2014 are entirely managed by the Grameen Foundation. The other partners backing these projects – DKT International, Marie Stopes, Concern Worldwide – do not have access to the platform and the associated database. The same is true in India, where the Indian Health Ministry and BBC Foundation, which oversee projects that use Motech, have to go through Grameen for any use of, or modification to, the platform.

On raising the various dysfunctions of Motech with the Grameen Foundation technical team, I was told that they were linked to the difficulty of maintaining the platform due to high turnover in the technical teams and the need to learn Motech's open-source code, which would therefore seem to be more complex than was suggested by the interviewee mentioned earlier. The Grameen Foundation recognises the difficulties of using the Motech code and has put training programmes in place for its own incoming teams, but has not as yet organised the transfer of skills to other project partners who will, however, ultimately be expected to take over the system, such as the Ghanaian or Indian health ministries. The 'technical skills deficit' for managing Motech can therefore be found among all the other Motech partners, be they Ghanaian, Indian or American. This is in effect a form of protectionism on the part of the Foundation, which has a certain expertise to sell and wants to stay 'in the business'. Open source is no guarantee of accessibility or of technology transfer, and without the transfer of the knowledge and knowhow associated with the software, it remains as impenetrable as any proprietary version.

### 3.3 Fencing in Interoperability

For Motech, as for other projects, the local actors do not have access to the technical part of the platform; they cannot modify the channel or even access the data they themselves collected. The Motech platform does not communicate with any other data platform. The data collected for Motech by the health workers is not interfaced with the national health information systems; it is stored and managed by the Grameen Foundation in silo mode. As a result, the health workers have to enter health data for Motech and then enter it again into the centralised health information system. This double entry operation is performed systematically, as the Motech register is oversimplified and does not include all of the information required by the central system on maternal and infantile health. Consequently, one observes two parallel data collection systems that do not communicate with each other and a double data entry process that takes up the precious time of the staff on the ground. This absence of interoperability and the low priority given to the data needs of national health information systems were criticised by several actors involved in Motech, both in Ghana and in India.

In Ghana, as in India, local technical teams and local technologies are systematically blamed by Motech's implementers for being late, closed, slow to adapt, less competent, and responsible for the lack of interoperability between the systems. Whereas in Ghana the centralised health information system did not yet exist when Motech was launched in 2010, India already had a national health information system when Motech arrived in 2012, and the Motech teams could have worked on it to ensure better communication between the two systems. However, the constantly changing standards for mobile platforms are decided a long way from Accra or Delhi, and the norms of Silicon Valley apply globally and unconditionally, on pain of being de-indexed by Google or Apple and thus no longer existing in the 'connected' world.

### 3.4 'Low-Cost' Technologies

The question of the cost of developing and maintaining the systems is another thorny issue. A platform such as Motech incurs multiple expenses, which the actors involved were always reluctant to quantify. When asked to detail the technical costs of the platform, they would never state a clear amount. Everything concerning the costs and expenditure of the Motech project, in India and in Ghana, remains opaque, and many transfers are not quantified, as they are sometimes skills transfers or service deductions. For the national project in India, the Gates Foundation has no contract or financial transaction with India's Ministry of Health. According to the ministry, however, a Motech project management team was installed at the ministry for three years at the expense of the Gates Foundation, which also covered all the costs associated with the launch of the national system as well as the development of the platform. These far from negligible costs are invisible and do not correspond to any official grant. In India and Ghana alike, it is impossible to have visibility on the revenues generated by the pay-to-use Motech applications (Kilkari and Mobile Midwife MTN). When asked about the revenues generated by these commercial applications, my respondents explained that the objective was not to make money and that the programme in any case costs far more than it brings in, though they were unable to say precisely what these costs are. The only transparent costs are the mobile connectivity charges announced by the pro-grammes' network operator partners. These costs merit closer analysis.

Focusing on Motech in Ghana, the cost of connectivity alone, that is access to the GSM network and the transfer of data over the network, is already a major barrier to the sustainability of the Motech project. The telecommunications market is dominated by multinationals from the Global North. In sub-Saharan Africa, for example, all the telecom groups with the exception of MTN (from South Africa) and Airtel (India) belong to developed countries (Ya'u, 2004). Ghana has no national telecom company; the sector is entirely privatised. It therefore pays the full rate, like many other countries of the South, for access to mobile telephony services. To provide pregnant women with free voice mes-sages, the Ghanaian state would, at the very least, have to cover the connectivity charges invoiced by the network operators. Nevertheless, financing connectiv-ity for Motech in Ghana presents an exorbitant cost for the government. The cost of sending out messages to the 9,000 women enrolled in the pilot district of Gomoa by itself amounts to 4,000 euros a month (paid for by the Gates Foundation), a cost that the ministry could not afford. If Motech were to be rolled out nationwide, the cost of sending voice messages to the target group of women would alone exceed 220 million euros a year. Of the thirty euros that the Ghanaian government devotes to the health of each Ghanaian woman every year, eight – almost a quarter of the total – would be spent on sending out a weekly Motech message. For the Ghanaian state, Motech is not an economical solution. It does not reduce general health expenditure; and here we are only considering the connectivity costs of the platform, which is just one of the mHealth cost items.

Instead of reducing healthcare costs, the low-cost promise of mHealth is turned on its head, and the Motech platform leads to spectacular inflation in the nation's healthcare costs. The funding required to operate mHealth proves to be significant for countries with limited financial resources to devote to health. The costs of digital development initiatives such as Motech are far from transparent, and the return on investment is made even harder to calculate by the fact that the impact of such initiatives is not evaluated clearly and independently. Moreover, even if the costs of Motech could be absorbed by the state, the integration of the platform into the national health system poses major questions due to its lack of interoperability and the various sticking points linked to mastery of the Motech source code, as discussed earlier.

The example of Motech highlights four mechanisms that amplify the technological inequalities between North and South. Firstly, the technical capabilities of the South are systematically doubted and put forward as a reason for the non-transfer of the knowledge required for the maintenance of the platforms. Secondly, blockages in the transmission of the supposedly open-source application code perpetuate forms of software ownership that are unfavourable to the South. Thirdly, interoperability between the systems from the North and those already in place in the South is impeded by a form of digital partitioning due to technical obsolescence, in terms of the standards defined by the North. Finally, the significant costs of the system – including, but not limited to, the amounts invoiced by the telecom multinationals – make it impossible for the state to finance the mobile platforms, as it is not always able to negotiate with the private operators. At first, both the Ghanaian and Indian governments agreed to implement the programme in selected pilot regions, as the technology was innovative and attractive, and because all costs were covered by the Gates Foundation. When they reached the end of the pilot phase, Ghana dropped out in 2015 and let Motech become a fee-based mobile service, sold by Ghana's leading mobile operator (MTN). The Ministry of Health pointed to the problems of ownership, interoperability and costs detailed earlier as major deterrents to expanding Motech nationwide. From 2016, India decided to enter a second pilot phase by expanding the programme from Bihar to five more Indian states – costs again borne by the Gates Foundation – and this phase is supposedly still ongoing.

The issues of international health governance linked to the new digital development model, and the trade-off decisions that need to be made, are all the keener now that health spending by governments of the South, as a share of their overall budget, is stagnating or even diminishing year on year. The example of Motech serves to illustrate how global priorities overshadow national goals and undermine the public health systems of the countries of the South by imposing technologies on them over which they have no control. Private actors from the Global North finance and pilot the programme, while public actors from the Global South provide their government staff to implement it on the ground, but have no access to the technical platforms and databases maintained by their own teams. This imbalance is facilitated by the ability to develop, manage and maintain digital tools remotely, and is reinforced by the innovative nature of the system, which calls for infrastructures and skills that are the automatic attribute of rich countries. Private stakeholders, seeking to position themselves as the sole technical experts capable of implementing these initiatives, block the transmission of technological knowledge and software-related skills, and maintain their monopolies. This distribution of roles also leads to a deterioration of local public health services, by diverting scarce and indispensable human resources towards mHealth projects whose usefulness is far from obvious. For mHealth entrepreneurs, the Global South is seen above all as a site for experimentation and as an untapped market for potential investment.

## 4 Datafication, Data Work and Data Management of Healthcare

The growing use of new digital healthcare technologies, within and outside healthcare infrastructures, has accelerated and intensified the production, circulation and usage of health data. Digital forms, online questionnaires and rating systems facilitate the collection and processing of feedback from internet or mobile phone users. 'Flash cookies' and 'smart' sensors collect data stealthily from browser histories or the activities of users of these technologies. A number of academic studies have shown that the digitisation of personal and health data in the Global North produces new forms of quantification, control and surveillance over people's lives (Haggerty and Ericson, 2000; Lupton, 2013; Lyon, 2011; Raley, 2013). Some have revealed that this sensitive data is used for commercial, governmental or administrative purposes often unknown to the patients or users of the systems who supplied the data (Gitelman, 2013; Lyon, 2014). Research into these questions in developing countries is scarce (Taylor and Schroeder, 2015). This section sets out to study how the digital data generated by mHealth in the Global South is collected (Section 4.1), protected (Section 4.2) and used (Section 4.3). The process of data collection – as other researchers have shown (Ribes and Jackson, 2013) – is often overlooked in discourse about digital technologies. That is as if the process were almost immediate, requiring no effort or skill; but nothing could be further from the truth. This section details the work of data production, collection, entry and transfer performed knowingly or unknowingly by health workers enrolled in the Motech programme. The primary objective of the 'datafication' made possible by Motech is to optimise the administration of healthcare. Using mHealth to achieve this goal means viewing health and healthcare from a particular angle, in which health data is a mode of management. From this perspective, the compilation, ownership and control of databases have crucial power implications. For Motech, community healthcare workers are both performing and enduring datafication at the same time.

## 4.1 Collecting Big and Small Data for Health in the Global South

In the connected world, data is the starting point for what we know, what we are and how we communicate. According to its advocates, Big Data and its analysis by 'smart' machines will make the world a better place; as Dominique Cardon explains, they claim that the calculations performed with this data *'can reduce administrative errors, medical approximations and market waste. Cross-referenced, made accessible, and opened up to algorithms, the data itself could then express things that were previously forbidden to it, or which remained hitherto unknown for lack of objective measurements. If our world is imperfect, it is because we don't have enough data to fix it'* (Cardon, 2015, 55). There is nothing new about the desire to 'datafy' the world in order to understand it better and improve it, but the means to achieve that goal, and the methods employed, have greatly evolved with digitisation and the processing power of computers. First let us examine what these 'data worlds' offer and encompass, what Big Data does for health and how it comes to be propelled into developing countries.

Data, big or small, is pursued enthusiastically by the advocates of digital health. 'Big Data', as it is known, collates a host of digital databases of different types on several populations, compiled from multiple, sometimes transnational and multilingual, sources (Ollion and Boelaert, 2015). There is nothing revolutionary about these demographic, social, economic, geographic or epidemiological data sets (Boyd and Crawford, 2012). It is their astronomical quantity, their continuous and even automatic generation, their aggregation and above all their common mode of analysis that make them something new and promising (Dagiral and Parasie, 2015). Big Data can be enriched by the less heralded 'small data', a subset of Big Data frequently used by the advocates of personalised healthcare. Small data is collected directly by individuals, either consciously, or unbeknownst to them, by new digital technologies. It can be used to track and monitor the user and sometimes to feed databases of Big Data (Neff, 2013). At the avant-garde of the collection and utilisation of small data we find the 'Quantified Self' (QS) movement, which measures and traces different aspects of daily life through 'smart' sensors and mobile applications (Lupton, 2013; Lupton and Jutel, 2015). Personal monitoring is not in itself anything new – athletes and diabetics have long kept diaries of their diet or physical activity – but the possibilities of automated monitoring, the ubiquity and the omnipresence of data collection instruments connected to or integrated into smartphones make such monitoring accessible and self-generated.

The datafication of the world is a recent global phenomenon, studied mainly in the Global North. Certain trends and certain questions raised by the work on the Global North are reflected in the Global South, where they sometimes come sharply into focus (Erikson, 2018; Mahajan, 2019). Inequalities of access to digital technologies are more marked in the Global South, and the traces generated by connected users in the Global South are far more limited quantitatively. Although mobile telephony has greatly increased connectivity in developing countries, barely 28 per cent of Africans used it for internet access in 2019, compared to 86 per cent of the inhabitants of developed countries (ITU, 2019). This gap raises many questions. If data is generated by internet connectivity, how can Big Data be representative of the poorly connected zones located mainly in developing countries? What happens when web-based automated data collection mechanisms cannot be used? In this context, does the mobile telephone have a particular role to play in the 'datafication' of the Global South?

Mobile telephony plays an important role in the 'datafication' of developing countries as it represents, in many development contexts, the sole and unique instrument of digital quantification. The lack of demographic and epidemiological data on the Global South is a major challenge for public health researchers and professionals (Jerven, 2013). The need for 'reliable' data, combined with a determination to cut the cost of producing statistics on the Global South, has spurred a host of new initiatives to make the collection of data on these less visible populations easier and less costly. Mobile phones consequently have a leading role to play in the planned 'datafication' of the Global South. To take the example of Ghana and India, where 23 per cent and 26 per cent of the population, respectively, use the internet, the mobile telephony penetration rate of almost 130 per cent (Ghana) and 79 per cent (India) holds out the prospect of much better statistical coverage by using the mobile telephone as a data collection device rather than web forms or online browsing histories. Additionally, mobile phones can generate geolocated data and can transmit data without going via internet networks (fibre or landlines), which are rare and costly in the Global South, by using text messages (SMS) or the even cheaper GPRS system. Data from mobiles makes fragments of the social visible; thanks to the obligatory registration and identification systems of SIM cards, users are now visible and identifiable. Forty-eight of the fifty-five countries on the African continent have adopted compulsory registration of SIM cards (Donovan and Martin, 2012), so much so that any active SIM card is now connected to an individual file containing data on the user. Where the resources and infrastructure to collect demographic data are cruelly lacking, mobile phones offer a new opportunity. The datafication of the Global South should therefore be seen alongside the generalisation of mobile telephony and the advent of applications capable of collecting data and communicating with remote platforms to analyse it (Taylor and Schroeder, 2015).

This evolution from simple geolocation to the collection of more social data by mobiles has led to the emergence of the very first studies on the Global South to make use of Big Data. One such study, for example, was carried out on 1.5 million mobile users in Rwanda, with the aim of demonstrating how to use the data generated by mobile operators to gain a better understanding of the behaviours of populations in developing countries (Blumenstock, 2012, 121). Rwanda's mobile penetration rate is currently around the 100 per cent mark, but the survey data go back to 2009, when the mobile penetration rate was only 24 per cent; indeed, the author warns about selection bias in the sample of people captured through mobile data: '*they tend to be wealthier, older, better educated, and are more likely to be male*' (Blumenstock, 2012, 121). Even a penetration rate of 100 per cent does not mean that the entire population has a mobile phone; it means that there are as many SIM cards in circulation as people in the population census. In Africa, as in South Asia, due to the segmentation of the telecoms market and the frequent network coverage problems, people sometimes use more than one SIM card to switch between operators (Cheneau-Loquay, 2012). Unequal access to mobile devices inevitably leads to biases in the data collected via this channel, rendering non-users invisible and over-representing the population groups captured by these forms of usage. Capturing population data via mobile phones therefore presents statistical limitations and raises questions about representativity.

Datafication in the Global South presents another particularity, in that it is often associated with development goals. The United Nations has set up an initiative, known as 'Global Pulse', to encourage the use of Big Data as an instrument for human development. According to Global Pulse, digital Big Data enables real-time evaluation of human situations and of the impact of development policies on their beneficiaries.[5] Big Data in the Global South, in particular, is used primarily for research projects and development programmes. However, this humanitarian mission statement should not be allowed to mask the role of private firms in this Big Data enterprise. In Global North and Global South alike, many huge databases are compiled by private commercial players. American geographers have shown that three quarters of the images used by the National Geospatial-Intelligence Agency come from commercial rather than government sources (Crampton, Roberts and Poorthuis, 2014), by which they suggest that decisions or analyses based on Big Data above all convey the viewpoints of those with the means and influence to compile, possess or access

---

[5] 'The initiative was established based on a recognition that digital data offers the opportunity to gain a better understanding of changes in human well-being, and to get real-time feedback on how well policy responses are working': website of the UN initiative, www.unglobalpulse.org, accessed on 20/07/16.

these databases. The few researchers working on Big Data in the developing world estimate – with reference to African cases – that digital data is supplied almost exclusively by private actors from the Global North (Taylor, 2015; Taylor and Schroeder, 2015). If Big Data comes with political and institutional objectives, and if it tends to be collected and used for particular ends, then the monopoly of private players from the Global North on Big Data from the Global South calls for scrutiny as to what control the populations thus made 'visible' have over their own personal data.

As Lisa Gitelman puts it: '*Raw data is an oxymoron*'; data does not exist spontaneously, it has to be generated, and the process of generation entails a substantial element of interpretation (Gitelman, 2013). It is primarily in the mode of collection and classification – how the data is ordered, separated out, reassembled and ranked – that the discreet and often invisible power of the 'datafication' of health, and of life, makes itself felt. Subsequently, the way the data thus assembled is used is a second, more visible, focus of power, already strongly critiqued in the Global North in general (Lyon, 2011; Mansell, 2011; Uimonen, 2016) and in the field of healthcare in particular (Lupton and Jutel, 2015; Wolf *et al.*, 2013). Far from being neutral, data accrues, depending on how it is collected, interpreted and used to support a particular position. In the field of information science, the concept of 'dataveillance' emerged in the 1980s to describe '*the systematic monitoring of people's actions or communications through the application of information technology*' (Clarke, 1988). Indeed data-driven surveillance predates IT: printed records or censuses are also techniques of biopolitical administration, and with a much longer history. David Lyon affirms that it is the degree, rather than the nature, of surveillance that changed with the advent of computer technologies, making pre-existing processes of control more effective, more widespread and less visible than before (Lyon, 2011). For Rita Raley, the difference is not only quantitative; surveillance practices may indeed be more widespread, but they are also of another order, as the intensification of data collection allows not only for new descriptive practices but also new predictive and prescriptive practices. Big Data offers a 'predictive optimisation' of life (Raley, 2013, 193).

mHealth, like other digital technologies, constructs a whole apparatus of surveillance and optimisation. It invokes the question of control on two levels, both as an object of medicine, and thus of political control over people's bodies, and as a technology of digital surveillance and supervision. Many mHealth initiatives – Motech included – promise healthcare optimisation through the implementation of two surveillance mechanisms: (1) the surveillance of patients, to reinforce compliance and limit 'defaulters', patients who fail to comply with prescriptions or courses of treatment; and (2) the surveillance of health workers, to check that they are dispensing the services asked of them, in the time allotted and with the means provided. By jointly optimising both patient compliance and health worker efficiency mHealth can, its advocates claim, improve the quality of the health system and above all achieve significant savings. To fulfil this optimisation objective, mHealth exerts a twofold surveillance over patients and health workers, one that is written into the very script of the system, that is into the uses for which the platform was designed (Akrich, 2010).

## 4.2 Data Protection and Privacy Issues

Any discussion of the mechanisms of 'dataveillance' via digital technologies necessarily entails, as a corollary, an examination of how the personal data thus collected is protected. The personal and omnipresent nature of the mobile phone raises new issues around the protection of privacy, which come into even sharper focus when its use is collective or shared, as it is in many countries of the South. Furthermore, the heterogeneity, multiplicity and dispersion of the actors involved in the transfer of this data increase the risk of error and of data 'leaks'. When it comes to the protection of personal data, the complex problems raised by mobile technologies are not specific to the field of mHealth, but they are amplified by the nature of the data involved. Health data are 'sensitive' and therefore require closer attention and tighter regulation. Whereas most countries have very strict laws on confidentiality and access to health data, the lack of legislation regarding health data on mobile phones seems all the more problematic, given that they facilitate the transfer and storage of data. The health-related use of mobile telephony forces us to ask still more searching questions about data security and respect for anonymity.

Many researchers have expressed serious reservations about data security, respect for confidentiality and privacy with regard to Big Data in the context of the collection and processing of globalised and de-territorialised health information (Bajwa, 2014; Bennett, 2011; Harvey and Harvey, 2014). Graham Greenleaf has examined all of the laws passed in this area over the last fifty years, starting with Sweden's Data Act of 1973, seen as the first law on data privacy (Greenleaf, 2014). He points out that in 2014, 101 countries (mainly the richer nations) had such laws, compared to only 8 (including Ghana) of the 55 countries in sub-Saharan Africa. The US and European legal systems have provided the model for the great majority of 'data privacy' laws, and yet these laws remain inoperative and fail to adequately protect the digital data of US and European citizens (Federal Trade Commission, 2013; European Union Commission, 2014). The European press regularly decries the leaking of personal data to commercial third parties.[6] Several researchers have shown that under these laws, anonymised data can easily be re-identified and attributed to specific individuals; they also criticise the consent forms which, when they are used at all, say nothing about the nature of the risks and the potential uses of personal data, and prevent users from withdrawing from the system later (Cardon 2015; Neff 2013). All of these studies converge to warn about the risk of abuse from the increasing surveillance of individuals by the digitisation of personal data without stricter privacy safeguards. Today, legislation on issues of confidentiality around mobile health data, while non-existent in many countries of the South, still remains fuzzy or unenforced even in the countries where is has been introduced.

India and Ghana both have legislation on personal data protection. India reformed its Information Technology Act in 2011 to include new provisions on the protection of personal data. The law in force nationwide applies to all Indian companies that 'collect, receive, possess, store, deal or handle personal data'. They are legally obliged to implement 'reasonable security practices and procedures' to protect such data and must formalise these measures in a confidentiality charter, indicating the type of personal data collected and the purpose for which it is to be used. All of these measures apply even if the information relates to persons outside India's jurisdiction. The Act stipulates that 'sensitive personal data' – particularly any information relating to people's physical and mental health, sexual orientation, medical records or biometric data – must be covered by the written and informed consent of the 'data provider' (the person or company supplying the data), and that the latter shall have the right to access, modify or withdraw the data at any time. The Indian framework also specifies the laws governing the transfer of data outside the subcontinent, and fines and penalties for infringing this regulation. I have no empirical data to confirm or disprove whether this legislation is effectively applied or complied with in India. India is one of the few countries of the South to have such precise legislation on digital data and to provide such protection for the consumer. The state of Bihar and the Government of India opted to retain responsibility for collecting data on pregnant women, whereas in Ghana it is handled by Motech. India's mother and child tracking system (MCTS) is entirely managed by the administration and is not accessible to the private third parties that administer the Motech platform.

The situation in Ghana is different. The country has a plethora of mHealth projects and the legislation, although reviewed only recently, seems to be

---

[6] Dredge, Stuart. 'Yes, those free health apps are sharing your data with other companies'. *The Guardian*, Technology section, 3 September 2013,. www.theguardian.com/technology/appsblog/2013/sep/03/fitness-health-apps-sharing-data-insurance.

inoperative. A Data Protection Commission was set up in 2012 by the Data Protection Act, passed the same year, in order to monitor its implementation. And yet, as this respondent laments, there are no regulation and control mechanisms in the country: *The main challenge is to put in place a regulatory mechanism for mHealth in this country. People don't want to talk about this but it's a real question. You need a good regulatory framework for mHealth. We have a data protection entity but it's not functioning, it doesn't know what is going on, it doesn't know who transmits what, which data is where; so if a project is ending, like Motech or Sharper, where do you keep that data? Who is responsible?* (H, UNAIDS, Accra, 07/14). My interviews with the telecom's regulation authorities and Data Protection Commission in Ghana confirm these concerns. The main mission of the Telecoms Ministry body, created by the Data Protection Act, is to draw up, on the basis of voluntary declarations, a register of companies that collect data digitally. According to the body's director, it has no budget of its own, and no controllers to check whether companies are toeing the line: '*We don't have a register for that yet; we don't have the means to check if they are complying with the law. And anyway, we don't have any direct enforcement powers. We've had a number of challenges with finances and setting up. For now we don't have any controllers, we need to raise money for that*'. Researchers working on the 'datafication' of the Global South observe the same type of problem in other countries. Linnet Taylor, who worked on the use of Orange customers' data in Senegal, states that the multiple laws are not applied, and that the only thing governing the exploitation of the data is the self-regulation exercised by the private firms or the researchers who process it (Taylor, 2015).

From the fieldwork in Ghana, it is clear that this self-regulation is not enough. The absence of regulation of personal data collection mechanisms and the multiplicity of intermediaries involved in mHealth programmes enable certain actors to make use of the data for commercial purposes. For example, the intermediaries in charge of sending out messages and attributing 'shortcodes' for the mHealth systems compile patient databases that they can then resell to other clients. The codes used for access to specific health messages carry data on their users and can be used to characterise them. Ghana's leading shortcode vendor made me an offer: I could buy a patient database for my communication campaigns, thanks to the data collected by the shortcodes used by mHealth applications: '*We have various ways of collecting the data: shortcodes, for instance, generate data. We have a database of 11 million subscribers categorised in various groups. So if you come to us and say you want to reach out to this target group of people, people in the health industry or in the health centres, we can look in our database and get you some numbers. Or you can come with a number of people you want to reach in that particular group and we'll look in our database to find you that volume'*. The shortcodes used by Mobile Midwife convey personal data (a mobile number that refers back to a user file) and a rough categorisation of mobile users (expectant or nursing mothers, depending on the code) to the provider, who can then commercialise a product derived from mHealth. The weak regulation of mHealth platforms allows private firms to market lists of contacts to third parties who want to reach particular consumers.

My work, following on from others, sheds light on how this data is produced, and how it engenders particular frames of interpretation depending on the context of its collection and use. To this end, I propose to study in detail the ways in which Motech data is quantified. I will then detail (in the next section) how it is employed to track the activities of the health workers and check that they are delivering healthcare. Motech's datafication process is essentially a response to healthcare administration management and optimisation objectives. Motech is therefore used as a technology for the supervision and digital surveillance of health workers and, through them, of patients. However, the mechanisms for obtaining feedback from patients and applying pressure to health workers are not at all the same. The automated sending of voice messages is not in itself a particularly restrictive mechanism for the women patients; after all, they can simply not answer the telephone, if they so wish. The control exerted by the technical platform over the female beneficiaries remains quite limited. Only the health workers can exercise effective control over the women's actions, by going out to meet them in the field. By contrast, Motech's datafication mechanisms enable effective control and surveillance of the CHWs, with the involvement of the health system managers in charge of healthcare administration (see Section 5). The filling in of forms, the listing of 'defaulters', the sending of reminders and alerts on services to be dispensed and so on are interesting illustrations of the 'dataveillance' put in place by Motech.

## 4.3 Agents and Objects of Datafication

In the field, data collection presents a number of obstacles. There are prerequisites: the health workers must be equipped with mobile telephones and must be able to use the applications. The Ghanaian case is particularly limiting, as the CHWs must not only have access to a mobile, and keep the same number for the duration, but they must above all have a device capable of running the Java script for Nurse's App. These conditions have proved impossible to reunite, and the programme has therefore had to supply mobiles so that the employees can use the application; however, these work-related telephones must remain at the

community or sub-district health centre. The managers of the Motech programme in Ghana speak of the additional constraints involved in supplying
and overseeing the fleet of mobile phones, even though it only concerns some
forty devices. The programme has also had to finance the monthly top-up fee of
all the mobiles using the Nurse's App, in order to ensure transmission of the data
to the Motech server. The problems around the use of mobile devices in rural
areas (network connection, phone credit or electricity) mean that the mobiles are
regularly unusable. This non-availability is further aggravated by the fact that
the mobiles must be kept at the health facility, instead of accompanying the
health workers on their visits to the villages, thereby taking the 'mobile' out of
the 'mobile phone' and making them even less accessible.

In India, data collection (which, as already mentioned, consists only of tracking
the activities of the CHWs) also faces several impediments. Although the applications can run on any type of telephone, the monitoring of the health workers
requires that they keep the same number for the duration. Whereas the mobile
penetration rate in rural India is lower than in Ghana, the CHWs, by virtue of their
healthcare activity, are nonetheless among the most 'connected' women in the
village. Even so, according to the block managers, almost 20 per cent of ASHAs
do not have regular access to a mobile phone. Unlike almost all of the AWWs –
who have a regular income, earning more than the ASHAs, and can therefore
absorb the expenses associated with mobile phone possession – the ASHAs do
not have the means. It was consequently seen as indispensable to pay for their
telephone minutes or provide compensation in the form of additional credit, in the
absence of other remuneration for their involvement in Motech. Two mechanisms
were put in place by the programme: free minutes for consulting Mobile Kunji
messages and 7 rupees (0.07€) credited on the CHW's mobile account for each
beneficiary enrolled in Kilkari for at least four weeks, with a further 7 rupees after
eight weeks. These incentives – a maximum of 14 rupees per enrolment – are
derisory when compared to the monthly telephone charges of 100–500 rupees (2
to 7€) paid by a CHW, the energy required to convince the beneficiaries to join
and remain signed up to the service, and the fact that the majority of the health
workers – the ASHAs – receive no fixed income. As one ASHA coordinator
explained: '*If I ask ASHAs to subscribe women for Kilkari, they tell me that they
would not do it for a meagre 7 rupees. They are right, because an ASHA doesn't
even get a salary. She is just on incentives. This requires her to walk to the
beneficiary's home, spend one hour, and at the end receive this little amount. It is
worth more than this*'.

Moreover, to receive the gratifications and free minutes associated with these
two mechanisms, the personnel must always use the same SIM card. As the Bihar
administration provides community health agents with neither telephones, nor

SIM cards, nor even phone credit, the block managers have to ensure that they give a stable reference telephone number so that their activities can be tracked in Kunji and Kilkari. These conditions are difficult to satisfy in certain districts of Bihar, as this block manager explains: *'I had to register mobile numbers of all ASHAs working in the area. They do not have a constant number, they keep changing them, or the mobile got lost'*. Most of the block officials criticise the limitations of the system when it comes to using mobiles in rural areas: *'In the field, she may not have her mobile all the time with her or the battery may be down. There may be no electricity; phones may not be available in the field'*. It fails to take account of the fact that, due to frequent problems with networks, phone credit or electricity, mobile telephony is not available to everyone, everywhere and at all times. The precondition of 'datafication' that consists in having a working and connected mobile seems, therefore, from these Ghanaian and Indian examples, hard to fulfil. Types of device, and access to the network, to electricity and to phone credit are all determining factors and make mobile telephony less ubiquitous and less reliable than such initiatives presuppose. This basic constraint of access to a mobile device jeopardised the operation of the whole programme. Nor is this the only obstacle: data collection also requires, for Motech Ghana, a data entry operator, and for Motech India, a user who leaves digital traces.

In Ghana, the professionals in charge of populating the Motech database, who are all trained nurses specialising in rural health, are literate and trained to fill in paper registers of information on antenatal visits, births and postnatal follow-up of mothers and newborns on a daily basis. This data entry task takes up a large part of their working day, but in return, it assists their clinical practice by facilitating the planning of community health centre supplies and activities. On top of this daily input routine, data compilation reports must be sent to the district every month. Nurse's App comprises, as we will see in detail in the following section, some fifteen input forms. However, using the mobile telephone to perform this work requires initial training as well as continuous practise so as not to forget the codes and file paths used by the system and, finally, demands a minimum incompressible amount of time to fill out all the forms. Unlike the district administrators, who have computers to enter the data from the paper registers every month, the CHWs' main digital input tools are their mobile phones. At the outset, the Motech project managers estimated that this significant change in practice would take a few months before becoming second nature. However, at the time of my fieldwork, after the CHWs had been using the application for over a year, input continued to pose a problem due to frequent issues with the mobiles, and the small size of the screens and keypads. The health workers find the Motech telephones unsuited to data collection: *'The phone is too small. The keys are too small when you are typing', 'The phones we are using, a lot of them are having problems. If you are bringing devices, please test it over and over before, to rule out the wrong ones and bring us only the right ones'.* Due to the device itself, and to the form-based structure, which requires dozens of successive screens just to enter the equivalent of one line of a paper register, digital data entry – even for practised users – takes a great deal of time. To cap it all, this long and painstaking task in no way dispenses the employees from filling in the paper registers, as the Nurse's App forms collect only a very limited part of the information regularly recorded in the registers; the paper version therefore continues to the be authoritative document.

In India, the obstacles to the smooth running of the project, as planned by its designers, are of another kind and relate particularly to the issue of literacy. The level of education and training of CHWs in India is significantly lower than in Ghana. AWWs are generally better trained and educated than ASHAs, but from one village to the next ASHAs have very variable educational levels, and some of them struggle to use the Kunji cards or the instructions for enrolling women in Kilkari because they can read only with difficulty. All of the block managers alluded to the problem of using tools that require written proficiency; they estimate that 20– 30 per cent of their ASHAs are illiterate: '*We have both educated and uneducated ASHAs. ASHAs who are educated can use Mobile Kunji actively. They would read out cards to the beneficiaries and use it. Some ASHAs are uneducated because even if the minimum eligibility criterion for ASHA is Std.8 qualified, in a few areas where we did not find any educated ASHAs, we had to select uneducated women too. Now, we can't remove these ASHAs and I have to work with everyone. Out of 229 ASHAs, 30 per cent are uneducated*'. The ASHAs, then, cannot always read the Mobile Kunji cards to the beneficiaries or use the shortcodes accordingly. Moreover, several administrators told me that some of the ASHAs' do not understand the voice messages and so cannot explain them to the beneficiaries due to the complexity of the language (Hindi) used as well as the content. While the Kunji and Kilkari applications do not require training in data entry for health workers, they do presuppose a sufficient educational level to be able to read the manuals and the Kunji cards. More than a quarter of ASHAs do not have a sufficient level of literacy to use them, and so are either excluded from the programme or pressed into participating in it without the minimum skills required.

Though presented as a time-saving optimisation tool for healthcare profes- sionals, mHealth in reality leads to an increase in human work rather than the opposite, as Nelly Oudshoorn has illustrated with regard to telemedicine (Oudshoorn, 2011, 190). In the context of the Motech project, the community health personnel encounter many difficulties and express multiple grievances with regard to the programme. These grievances – from the health workers and their supervisors – constitute additional 'traces' of usage, attesting to the numerous limitations or even basic problems with the platforms, but also to conflicts around the very concept of what 'taking care' of somebody actually means. Firstly, these technical dysfunctions are regularly put forward as the main cause for the health workers' low level of engagement with, or even disengagement from, the programme. They report problems with the device itself: 'Sometimes *the phone freezes when you are uploading forms'*, or to do with charging the battery. All of the districts I visited in India and Ghana are supposedly 'covered' by several mobile networks, but all of the health professionals I met have daily problems with connectivity: '*The ASHA would go to the beneficiary and read the appropriate card to them, when they try the number given on the card, the number comes engaged. It says "all lines to this route are busy." This happens quite a lot'*. The staff also signal the numerous problems with messages from the Motech database that the patients report to them. Some, in the Indian case, do not receive the messages, even when credit is debited: '*They ask us to stop this service because money keeps getting deducted but they do not get calls'*. Other patients do not receive the messages intended for them: '*Sometimes the clients received always the same message over and over and not any other messages. The same unique message all the time'*. When things go wrong, most of the patients hold the community health agents liable, as they were responsible for signing them up to the service. Other technical problems have a direct impact on their activity.

In Ghana, the professionals have no confidence in the reminder system because they receive reminders for patients who are not in their district or because they see women arriving at the health centre after receiving reminders even though they were not supposed to come. The already overburdened CHWs are not lacking in motivation; what they lack are tools that they can rely on in order to perform their tasks. The recurrent technical dysfunctions end up turning them away from Motech. They point out that the errors it generates represent, at best, a source of dissatisfaction, and at worst a risk of professional malpractice that could result in patient harm. These criticisms contrast starkly with mHealth's promise of efficiency and constitute a major barrier to its adoption. Some dysfunctions, such as the routing of messages, can be corrected; others, such as connectivity, require heavy investments that mobile operators are reluctant to fund in remote and seemingly unprofitable areas.

In addition to the aforementioned technical problems, the health personnel identify limitations inherent in the very structure of the programme as deployed. Some of them contest the rules or the principles of incentivisation contained in the scheme. Several managers state that the compensation mechanisms for the involvement of the community health agents are incommensurate with the time invested:

'*The time of the people involved is important, if a nurse is using 20* per cent *of her time for mHealth, how is she rewarded for that time?*'. In the Indian case, several administrators feel that the system of compensation after four weeks of enrolment in Kilkari is unfair and fails to reflect the agents' commitment: '*I feel that the ASHAs should get incentives for starting the service, not for continuation of the service. They worked and tried for it and also invested their time and energy and they mobilised the beneficiaries, but won't get anything for that*'. Some criticise the multiplication of rival mHealth systems and their lack of interoperability. They mention using several mobile telephones for several mobile applications in parallel:

> *You have different phones running different applications at the same time, you can have 4 or 5 phones at the same time, which could be a problem. At the facility level, there are only few people who are running those many applications. It's time-consuming and even confusing, if you have to run different systems. The idea was that when you fill a register through the mobile you won't have to do it on the paper; this has not worked for Motech.*

The lack of interoperability between the different collection tools, added to the lack of reliability of the data entered and the reminders, constitutes a major barrier to the acceptance of these systems by the already overworked professionals, as confirmed by an official from the Ghanaian Ministry of Health: '*If you come with a system that cannot integrate into the existing system, you will still keep rolling it out and you will still burden the community health workers*'. The actors encountered unanimously say that the multiplication of distinct collection tools makes for extra paperwork and less time for healthcare.

The professionals interviewed clearly see the usefulness of having mobile telephones for their work: sending a message to patients or co-workers can save them a journey; electronic diaries or reminder systems can help them get organised. These far from negligible aids assist them in their work, but all the professionals stress the lack of basic working tools essential to their practice, which mobile phones can never make up for: access to clean water, soap, disinfectant products, vaccines, medicines, cotton wool, a bag to hold it all in and a means for transport for getting to the communities. Several professionals encountered during training sessions on new, latest-generation Android smart-phones or on digital tablets felt that the money used to finance these techno-logical gadgets could have been used to solve some of their day-to-day difficulties by investing in other more traditional tools or by training more professionals in healthcare practices.

These grievances, and these difficulties in implementing mHealth programmes, can be understood as criticisms of the new technophile priorities or modes of organisation conveyed by mHealth, which overlook basic needs, rather than as mere technophobia or generational incompetence on the part of workers or supervisors easily dismissed as change-resistant. The health professionals welcome and roll out the mHealth initiatives in their districts, but they question the reliability of the platforms, and their impact on their practice and on the care delivered to the beneficiaries. Their involvement in mHealth depends on the ability of these programmes to propose solutions to their day-to-day problems. What the Motech applications propose is essentially a set of quantification methods oriented towards healthcare administration. The inadequate or, for that matter, highly coercive compensation systems instil dynamics that seem to enjoy little support from the health professionals who are so indispensable to the implementation of these projects. Section 5 will address what becomes of the data and how it is used. The Motech programme's use of data shows that assemblages of this type are above all managerial innovations, new techniques of public health administration.

## 5 Optimisation and Performance Management of Healthcare Workers

Health professionals play a pivotal role in mHealth, contributing to the roll-out and sometimes the implementation of projects. They also represent a target for initiatives aimed at improving their practice. For Motech, the health professionals in question are the CHWs. They raise awareness among end users, register them and enter the health information required for the operation of the Motech platform. In return, the platform promises greater work efficiency, thanks to the automation of certain tasks, the digitisation of health data to facilitate collection and analysis, the reception of alerts and, finally, better organisation and work planning. I met with some 120 health professionals involved in mHealth projects in Ghana and in India, including some 20 CHWs who had been using Motech for over a year in Ghana, and 30 who had been using it for almost two years in Bihar. I was therefore able to study the dual perception of these workers as both agents and 'beneficiaries' of the Motech data collection system. I also met with some twenty managers in charge of supervising the health workers using Motech. These interviews enabled me to understand the managerial issues and organisational constraints involved in mHealth.

### 5.1 Optimising Healthcare Management Through Mobile Data

Through the example of the Motech applications used by the health workers – the Nurse's App in Ghana and Mobile Kunji in Bihar – I propose to examine different ways of collecting data over the same mobile platform. In the

Ghanaian case, the health workers voluntarily collect health data to improve their practice; in the Bihari case, data is collected automatically by the Mobile Kunji and Kilkari applications, unbeknownst to the health workers, in order to monitor their activities. I intend to examine the discourses and arguments in favour of this form of collection, and the prerequisites and conditions for its implementation. I will also touch on health workers' reactions to this collection and how the data is used by their managers. The analysis will therefore contrast the perceptions of the Motech administrators with those of the health professionals involved, and compare the discourse about the managerial innovations made possible by mHealth with the constraints and difficulties of its implementation.

With respect to data collection, the Ghanaian and Indian versions of Motech are very different. In Ghana, the application dedicated to data collection – the Nurse's App – plays a role every bit as important as the one for sending messages to pregnant women (Mobile Midwife). The two applications are presented and given equal prominence in all of the documentation. From its launch, the Motech project has had these two sides to it. It is therefore easy to find statements explaining and justifying the data collection process in Ghana. The situation is very different in Bihar, as the module for data collection by health staff and the forms for completion on mobile phones were not retained for the Indian version of Motech. India already has its own MCTS, managed by the central and state administrations, which does not communicate with Motech. Nevertheless, the aim of leveraging data to optimise healthcare administration through the use of Motech has not disappeared from the programme. The Kilkari and Mobile Kunji applications also hold out the promise of closer control and surveillance of health staff, based on the traces left by using the systems.

In Ghana, Motech includes – alongside Mobile Midwife – Nurse's App, a health data collection system that enables health professionals to create a dossier on a patient. The system then allows the patient to be registered with Mobile Midwife and generates a unique authentication code that can be used to identify her in the Motech database. Once this dossier has been created on the application, the professional, after each visit, completes the health data forms (mForms), which are stored on the telephone, and transmits them to the Motech server where the patients' personal medical records are centralised. The health workers can consult the database to obtain a list of patients who have missed appointments or who are due to give birth during the week. Every week, the system sends the health workers an alert message to remind them of their tasks. It also enables district health managers to generate monthly reports using the data collected.

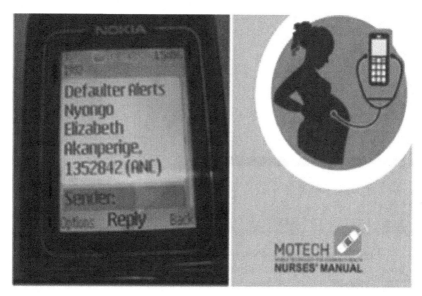

**Figure 4** Mobile phone and manual issued to CHWs by Motech Ghana
**Source:** Grameen Foundation: https://grameenfoundation.org/documents/5ozoc8 ste2hjjkxekff8.pdf

The collection system is explained in a manual given to the health workers by the Grameen Foundation when they are trained to use Motech. With the application, the employees create health dossiers on the women. They can consult or add to the system over their mobile phones. The dossier contains information on age, place of residence, number of children, number of pregnancies, a reference telephone number and the status thereof (public/family/husband's/own telephone), the National Health Insurance Scheme (NHIS) number and the subscription expiry date. There are some fifteen different forms in the application that the personnel can use to either consult or add to the Motech database.

Some of these mForms can be used, for example, to collect the number and dates of the patient's antenatal visits, information on the birth – date, place, whether a health worker was present, any complications that arose – and so on. Likewise, there are forms concerning postnatal visits for mother and infant, but also to report the various illnesses – malaria, tetanus, diphtheria, chicken pox, and so on – that can affect the patients or their newborns, and any vaccinations administered. Other forms are provided to register the death of a Motech patient or her child, cases of miscarriage and new pregnancies. The explanatory manual systematically takes the example of the paper registers to illustrate how to complete the mForms with clinical data. To enrol a new patient, using the dedicated enrolment form in Mobile Midwife to enter the patient's language

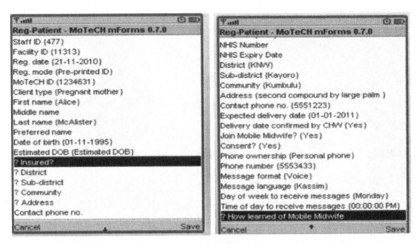

**Figure 5** Fields to be completed when enrolling a Motech client
**Source:** Grameen Foundation: https://grameenfoundation.org/documents/5ozoc8
ste2hjjkxekff8.pdf

preference and preferred time for receiving messages, the user must complete thirty-one successive screens. Two sample screenshots of the form are shown in Figure 5, but they represent the demonstration screen and not the screen actually used by the staff, which is the much smaller one seen above.[7] There is also a form for unsubscribing from Mobile Midwife.

In every case, the health worker must start by saving the form on his or her telephone and then subsequently – once there is adequate network coverage – sending the forms thus saved to the Motech database, at which point the system flags up which forms are accepted and which are rejected on account of input errors or failure to complete required fields. A properly completed dossier is a precondition for the enrolment of the beneficiaries in Mobile Midwife, and for receiving reminders of upcoming visits. Motech Ghana, meanwhile, aggregates the results of all the completed forms from the different Community Health Planning & Services (CHPS) zones in a district, to generate monthly reports: reports that can be used by managers to evaluate the outreach work of CHWs in their district.

The Motech database can be interrogated in two ways. At the scale of their work area (the CHPS zone), staff can be sent text messages with the various lists of 'defaulters' in their zones, that is patients who have missed an appointment or have not had a particular vaccination, as well as the list of upcoming, recent or overdue births. At the scale of the patient's personal file,

---

[7] To view the Grameen Foundation's demonstration video for Nurse's App, see: https://youtu.be/ Fw_PwiT-ZmY

they can consult for upcoming dates, visits and vaccinations by entering the patient's Motech identification number, NHIS number, reference telephone number or date of birth. Nonetheless, all interactions between CHWs and their line supervisors continue to go through paper registers. Only in a few isolated cases do CHWs interact digitally with the district health manager, as one Grameen employee told me: *'Nurses record the patient data into mForms but they have paper registers that are replicas of those mForms'*. In Ghana, digital interactions between Motech and the health staff are therefore limited to the forms filled in over the telephones by the health workers, to the corresponding alerts that the system then sends out and to the reports that the district health managers can generate on the Motech web platform. Interactions between staff and supervisors still rely on paper registers. However, the collection of data will play a role in organising the work of the community health agents, and in spurring competition between them.

Motech's data collection mechanism in India is much less 'transparent' than Nurse's App. It features in no document or manual, and is nowhere to be found in the official communications on the Indian programme, as it does not rely on the voluntary collection of data by CHWs. It comes to light only through fieldwork with health workers, Motech administrators and sub-district managers. The Motech platform can generate a great deal of data, from the shortcodes used to listen to Mobile Kunji messages or from enrolments in and usage of Kilkari. As an Indian technician of the project explained to me, the automatic tracking of the usage of Kunji and Kilkari generates dashboards that consolidate particular analyses of these data traces:

> *We could look at many different indicators, which shortcodes are more used, how long on average people are listening to the calls, from which districts the majority of the calls are dialled in and dialled out, for how long have they been using the service, how many total minutes have been consumed, how many calls have they answered or not, how many people have received incentives, how many new subscribers.*

The project managers in Bihar present this collection mechanism as a way to optimise their community health work by monitoring the actions of the health workers, known in India as ASHAs, AWWs or FLWs (Frontline Workers). The number and duration of 'outreach' home visits can be deduced from the shortcodes dialled on the health worker's mobile and associated with the Mobile Kunji cards, as one Motech employee in Bihar attests:

> *Mobile Kunji is a way of monitoring outreach, that's what we tell them. Because as of today they cannot monitor outreach. Your FLW is giving self-reported data saying I've been to this many households this month, but you*

*are not able to verify it. This system is a way to verify that. With Mobile Kunji*
*you can track usage through the phone number. So the trained FLW registered*
*her number; every time she uses it, we get to know which card she used, the*
*duration of usage. We are able to track all those things over there. It's a way*
*to know if and how those household visits are happening.*

The number of beneficiaries enrolled in Kilkari by each FLW and their length of subscription to the service constitute another type of data collected and used for visibility on home visits and on work performed, since Kilkari subscribers are necessarily attached to a health worker's telephone number, as another employee in Delhi explains: '*When a beneficiary is subscribing to Kilkari he is always reporting the number of an FLW that referred him. They need to give that number otherwise they don't subscribe. . . .We deal with the incentives to the FLW. We track that based on the eligible criteria, if an FLW is supposed to get incentives, the system will generate a report, and we'll load the credit on her number*'. The data generated by Motech Bihar therefore comes from traces of usage of Mobile Kunji associated with FLW telephone numbers, and from subscriptions and durations of use of Kilkari by the beneficiaries attached to each health worker. This data, collected without the knowledge of the women who use the applications, is used for the purpose of supervising their work and, among other things, for remunerating completed tasks.

## 5.2 The Policy of the Carrot and the Stick!

The Motech administrators have put incentive systems in place, with the district and block managers, to promote the use of the applications and the collection of data. Two different but not mutually exclusive approaches have been taken by the actors I met in India and Ghana. The Ghanaian managers have tried to encourage emulation between health workers by creating competition between them, offering 'rewards' for their level of participation in Motech. The Indian version, less 'engaging' at the outset for the CHWs, has proved to be more coercive and restrictive for the women whose supervisors took on the 'dataveillance' function proposed by Motech.

In Ghana, the Motech collection process cannot, as we saw, replace the paper registers, and so inevitably represents an additional task, even if the professionals acknowledge the usefulness of the reminders in anticipating healthcare demand: '*We get to know our defaulters from the messages; that's important for us. It helps for planning outreaches, it will give you some estimates, you'll know how many people you'll have to immunise, so you can prepare for that particular injection so you are not short of vaccines*'. After more than a year of entering health data in Motech, however, despite their familiarity with the forms, they are highly critical of the system. Unanimously, they describe collecting data on mobiles as a time-consuming extra workload compared with the paper registers of the national system: '*You still have to register in the paper book, so it takes more time than the normal data collection. And sometimes after work, you still work on the Motech, you have to do uploads and registration on the phone*', though the promise of saving time, thanks to the reminders and the automated sending of monthly reports to the district, was initially the sole incentive for collecting Motech data.

In response to these observations, the project administrators sought other ways to incentivise data collection. Firstly, they set digitisation targets for the health centres, giving them 'automation goals' to achieve every month for the generation of the monthly district reports. All the community agents in the sub-district were supposed to complete a cumulative total of 80 per cent of the required mForm data. In reality, no single employee can fill in all of the forms needed for the district report: some handle the antenatal follow-up forms, others the pathology forms. At each facility, there is a division of labour between datafication and data entry. Here again, how-ever, the system of shared targets for each facility has been seen as penalising the workers who fill in the mForms. An employee may complete all of her allotted data, but if other employees in the facility fail to do so, the shared target is not met. In several districts, a system of individual rewards was consequently introduced for the workers uploading the most data to the Motech server, with quarterly gratifications in the form of foodstuffs (rice, powdered milk, biscuits) for the top performers, and T-shirts or Motech-logo certificates for the runners-up. However, this system of incentives to recog-nise individual workers was once again strongly criticised by the healthcare personnel and abandoned in certain districts, as it had the effect of rewarding administrative tasks rather than clinical work.

In their 'lessons learned' report, the Motech Ghana project managers express a clear concern for improving health worker buy-in, and address the issue from two angles: on the one hand, they suggest a bonus scheme with the introduction, from the launch of the project, of a reward system in the form of free minutes of phone credit or mobile-related gifts (solar-powered chargers, etc.); on the other, they consider that the system needs to be more coercive, under the authority of the CHWs' employer, so that the CHWs see Motech as an integral part of their work rather than as a temporary external imposition: '*Having an intervention introduced by the users' employer makes them more likely to adopt it as part of their existing work and accept it as a change to their existing work, rather than additional work for an outside entity. This is important in encouraging adoption and compliance*' (Grameen, 2012, 54).

The incentive to use the applications, based on free or additional phone credit, was introduced from the outset for the Motech project in Bihar. However, this 'carrot' was apparently insufficient to inspire widespread use of Mobile Kunji or Kilkari. As a result, the Motech administrators in India made use of the data generated by the applications to impose a more coercive policy.

According to my interviews, the Indian block managers preferred to use intimidation rather than rewards, as attested by this manager, keen on applying 'pressure' to push CHWs into using Motech: '*So, I gave them some time and deadlines to improve, kept pressurising them periodically that they have to do it*'. More generally, the managers use data generated by Kilkari and Kunji to administer community healthcare remotely, since they cannot go into the field to check the work of the hundreds of workers under their supervision. From the minutes used for Kunji, they deduce the number of home visits made:

> *Mobile Kunji is like a key which I got which gives me a rough figure of number of such home visits made by ASHAs in terms of number of minutes used. If the message is one minute long, and she visits one beneficiary, one minute will be used. So, I get to know which specific cards have been used for how many minutes. I use this data to monitor them. I get to know how much work has been done. I am also physically verifying in the field but there are 301 ASHAs in this block and I can't go physically to all of them. At the maximum I can monitor 20–25 ASHAs in a month.*

Some managers judge the quality of the health workers' performance by the yardstick of the quantity of subscriptions to Kilkari: if they don't succeed in signing beneficiaries up to Kilkari, then they are not effective in their interactions: '*The data is available for each ASHA. We know their number of subscriptions to Kilkari along with the incentives credited to them. If some ASHA is not performing well, I try to visit her area with her. . . . It is not that people do not want to subscribe to Kilkari, it depends upon inter-personal communication and how you are convincing the beneficiary*'. Others share that they use consolidated Motech data for each village (panchayat) at the monthly team meetings to exert constant pressure on CHWs and 'push' them to perform better:

> *We do not use individual data for each ASHA, we use a percentage of ASHAs and AWWs actively using Mobile Kunji in one particular panchayat. Let's say we take panchayat P: we have 10 AWWs there . . . .. In any programme if there are 10 people who are self-motivated, there will always be 5 who have to be pushed. Continuous tracking helps.*

These new mHealth-based control mechanisms change the nature of the control exercised over the workers. The ubiquitous dimension of this control – the illusion that the system controls everyone individually everywhere at once, inexorably and infallibly – represents Motech's 'added value'. Some of the supervisors explain that because Motech is not based on self-declaration, it is more credible and reliable, obliging the workers to tell the truth about their work, because any false claims will be found out: '*ASHAs feel that we have individual data for each ASHA and if they lie, they will be caught*'. This surveillance can have significant consequences for the workers, especially for the ASHAs: being 'paid' per intervention, their precarious status makes them even more vulnerable when faced with such surveillance mechanisms. The supervisors assess them on the basis of the call minutes used for Kunji and threaten to replace them if they do not use up all of their minutes: '*Currently, we are assessing their performance based on the number of minutes they are able to use. We tell them that they have to finish their minutes, or they have 50 per cent of the minutes remaining. . . . We warned them also that they can be removed if there were serious issues, to create pressure*'. According to these supervisors, the Motech system promotes accountability among health workers, spurring them to be more effective. This type of management system was unanimously rejected by health workers, based on the multiple difficulties in accessing mobile-based services in rural India, where connectivity as well as ownership of mobile phones among women is very low (Al Dahdah and Kumar, 2018).

Certain supervisors point out that accountability mechanisms were already in place before the advent of Motech. At block level, the field visits or the monthly team meetings already provided some visibility on the work performed; the paper registers and the visit calendars that the health workers have to complete were already used as management tools by the supervisors: '*We have informal information about ASHAs and their performance. We also have different other reports too which help us understand whether ASHA is working or not*'. These supervisors, more critical of the Motech system, feel that the analysis of the Motech traces does not constitute a more reliable tool than the reports, and is not sufficient for managing the teams. In their view, the paper registers and visit schedules enable them to monitor the activities of the health workers: '*We verify the number of home visits that she made, from entries in her home visit planner. If she did not go to these people, we would get to know*'. They emphasise that the automated system for collecting traces of Motech usage can be evaded just as easily as the self-declaration system and cannot guarantee that the visit actually took place: '*Even if we have the data, physical verification is necessary. Suppose, I may call the given numbers, sitting at my home. Whether the ASHA is actually going to the beneficiary for her visit or not, this monitoring is essential*'. They consequently refuse to use these applications to penalise the community health auxiliaries, arguing that they can do a good job without necessarily relying on these tools:

*Many ASHAs are not educated. We cannot expect such ASHAs to use Mobile Kunji and also Kilkari sometimes. There are 135 ASHAs out of which 20 per cent are not educated. What do we do? We trained them because that is what we have in our hands. They are able to mobilise people, they may be vocal and are doing other work well but they cannot do Mobile Kunji.*

They also point out that the non-usage of services may be attributable to technical factors such as network problems, where the consumption of additional mobile credit by the service has left the workers in financial difficulty. These reasons, beyond their control, justify the non-usage of a service seen as defective: '*According to the data, we review them and ask for the reason for non-usage. Some say that due to network problems, the number does not get connected. Sometimes, the credit from an ASHA's mobile is deducted*'. Finally, a number of supervisors refuse to hold the CHWs alone accountable for the community health services, judging that their responsibility is also engaged, and that their way of organising the work and their relations with the health workers are equally crucial to smooth health service delivery: '*I also review ASHAs on a monthly basis. Through this review, I am able to assess whether they are performing well or more support is required to them. I never tell them that they did not perform well. If they did not, I think that somewhere we did not do our work nicely*'.

The introduction of a coercive policy to implement the 'dataveillance' proposed by Motech therefore depends on the convictions of the block managers. Some of them have no problem with viewing the traces of Motech usages as reflecting the activity of the health workers and in penalising them on the basis of the data transmitted by the systems, while others remain unconvinced by this mode of management. The survey does not allow us to establish in what proportions the block managers follow or resist this management system at the scale of Bihar state (in the blocks studied, 40 per cent of supervisors refused to use the Motech traces as a management tool). The Motech administrators, conscious of the key role of the block managers in the adoption of the platforms, consequently decided to change the way Motech is implemented. In the first districts, they themselves trained the FLWs to use Motech, with little involvement from the block community managers (BCMs). Now it is the BCMs who are trained and who in turn train the health workers, as I was told by a Motech employee: '*In the eight innovation districts where the programme was first launched, we trained ourselves the FLWs. But when we moved out of the eight innovation districts, we involved the BCMs and trained them so that they will train the FLWs. And the usage of those new districts is much higher, because of the involvement of the BCMs*'. In so doing, the Motech administrators have a better chance of persuading the supervisors of the usefulness of the data and the 'dataveillance' it makes possible.

Data-driven health, with its quantifications and its predictive models, proposes to optimise health systems. It promises to remedy the dysfunctions that affect the systems of the Global South and the Global North with the help of calculations, indicators and algorithms to meet the needs of populations without wasting resources. The objective of this section was to understand how health workers and facility managers appropriate this model – if indeed they do – and how they make use of the quantification data. The field analysis illustrates the prerequisites and practical constraints with which health actors in the Global South are faced when it comes to the datafication of their activities. Though it may seem straightforward, the Motech system in practice requires access to working mobile phones with a stable and uninterrupted connection, which is by no means a given in the rural areas of the countries studied. To perform data collection, the system in Ghana requires particular mobile phones, which had to be supplied to the health workers. Moreover, in both Ghana and India, the health workers have to be trained to use the applications. The use of Motech's clinical databases is perfectly opaque, and the public health services do not have access to it; the survey could therefore not identify any use of this data other than for administrative and managerial purposes by the Motech actors.

Data collection is often perceived as superfluous or even detrimental by the health workers themselves, who feel undermined by mechanisms that are designed to monitor rather than support their practice. This sentiment is reinforced by the fact that the data collected by Motech is not linked to the centralised health information systems in either India or Ghana and so cannot be used by the professionals to manage stocks of medicines, for example, or to identify a listed practitioner who can take charge of a patient who they cannot treat. The manager of a health centre in Ghana summed it up thus: '*We don't need those data here and there anymore. We need more resources. We need more nurses. We need more drugs and more commodities*'. For these professionals, data collection, disconnected from their practice, consumes more resources than it generates benefits. This 'datafication', in their view, makes for more work and less time, time that should be devoted to what they see as their core activity: taking care of the population. Big Data is valuable and useful only in particular contexts and for particular systems; the decontextualisation of information – presented as its great strength – in practice guarantees that it will not be able to address the difficulties of clinical practice, because it only sees the 'big picture'.

## 6 Intersecting Technological Inequalities

The advocates of Motech promote the platform as a tool of empowerment for women, a means of compensating for gender inequalities – a discourse echoed by the local and international media, as typified by the article headline '"Mobile Midwife" Empowers Ghanaian Women'.[8] This claim of empowerment resonates strongly with the perceptions of the various Motech actors, be they supporters or beneficiaries of the system, enabling some to justify the implementation of Motech and others to reveal its limitations.

This section studies the gender relations at work in Motech and the way in which the programme proposes new reassignments by positioning the mobile phone as a means of empowerment and of compensating for gender inequalities. The investigation reveals that mobile phone usage is gendered. Women, as with other technologies, are under-equipped when it comes to mobile phones. Several feminist studies have indeed shown that access to digital technologies is generally more difficult for women (Wyatt, 2005). Presented as a key tool of empowerment, the mobile telephone has turned out to be – in Ghana and in Bihar alike – an instrument of male domination, and its usage goes to the heart of gender inequalities. Far from being a lever of emancipation, it reinforces the male dominance already in place and further confines women to the home. However, the analysis goes beyond this observation and shows, through comparative analysis, how the Motech programme confirms, amplifies or mitigates domination and inequality. It shows, for example, how the care–giving relationship is transformed by the introduction of the system.

## 6.1 The Mobile Phone, an Instrument of Male Domination

Maternal health is one of the areas of healthcare automatically associated with women; pregnancy and caring for young children remain a woman's 'privilege' in most parts of the world (Potvin and Frohlich, 1998). In my regions of study, moreover, the workers in charge of maternal and infantile health are almost exclusively women, the role of the men being limited essentially to that of financial provider (Bhat, 2015). In Ghana, some women cited their husbands as an important source of support during pregnancy, but in Bihar no woman said she had been helped by her husband during this period. In the rural areas of Ghana and Bihar, maternal health is still very much a 'woman thing' and Motech, it seems, is no exception to the rule.

In Bihar, very few women are reached by the programme, and most of the women enrolled in Motech have listened to fewer than four messages; barely a dozen were able to recall even the gist of the messages, and none could remember the content precisely. The multi-sited investigation enabled me to

---

[8] NextBillion.net: '"Mobile Midwife" Empowers Ghanaian Women'. http://nextbillion.net/blogpost .aspx?blogid=3639. Consulted on 17 December 2013.

understand why so few women sign up for Motech and why most of them unsubscribe after listening to just a few messages. In India, the two main reasons for not subscribing or for unsubscribing from Kilkari are the difficulty of access to a mobile phone and the cost of the service, as these women explained: *'I didn't sign up because my husband takes his mobile with him to work; how could I listen to the messages?'*; *'Paying one rupee per message is too much for me'*. Analysis of unsubscription from the service reveals conflicts between men and women, unequal gender relations and clear cases of male domination, as illustrated by these verbatims: *'My husband said there was no need to listen to the messages and that the money was deducted. He wasn't prepared to understand when I tried to persuade him.'*; *'My brother told that a lot of money was deducted by the service, so he deactivated it. He told me he wouldn't let me use the mobile any more from now on'*. As Kilkari is a paid service, and the mobile penetration rate in rural India is much lower than in Ghana,[9] the Indian case offers a 'close-up' of domination at work in mHealth programmes. Access to a mobile is particularly difficult for young Indian women in rural areas, but the Ghanaian situation offers many parallels, and the gender inequalities are similar in Ghana.

Seen through the prism of gender, the reasons for not subscribing to or for unsubscribing from the service are all linked to issues of male domination. In practice, the (male) 'head of household' (husband, brother, uncle or father-in-law, depending on the family set-up) finds the service too expensive, or unnecessary, and refuses to let the woman subscribe, does not lend her his mobile or does not top it up with enough credit for access to the service. Whichever case applies, the role of the head of household is key; it is he who refuses to pay for the service or who decides to terminate it. The Motech study illustrates, in this respect, male control over 'legitimate' uses of mobile technology by women.

Being less costly and easier to use, mobile telephones are often seen as more 'egalitarian' than other communication technologies.[10] And yet a woman in the countries of the South will be 14 per cent less likely than a man to own a mobile phone, a gap that rises to 38 per cent if she lives in South Asia and is higher still in rural areas.[11] Mobile access is therefore a critical issue for women across the Global South, but the gender gap is far more marked in India than in Ghana. The Bihar example is therefore particularly symptomatic of the gender inequalities

---

[9] 48 per cent in Bihar vs. 130 per cent in Ghana in 2015 at the time of our study.

[10] On this topic, see the ITU and UNESCO report: 'Doubling digital opportunities: enhancing the inclusion of women and girls in the information society'. (Geneva: UNDP, September 2013).

[11] GSMA report: 'Women & Mobile: A Global Opportunity. A study on the mobile phone gender gap in low and middle-income countries', January 2013.

and male domination linked to mobile telephony. While the situation is less acute in Ghana, the same background trends are also in evidence there.

In this investigation, women with their own mobile phones are overrepresented relative to the general population, as they were the main target for subscription to the Motech service. In Ghana, 80 per cent of the women encountered had their own phones, compared with 50 per cent in Bihar. In the Ghanaian sample, almost all of the women in paid work had their own mobile phones. In Bihar, none of the women were in paid employment, but 70 per cent of those with their own phone had husbands working outside the state. Having an income of one's own, and/or husband living far away from the village are therefore factors that facilitate the acquisition of a mobile phone.

As well as the ownership of the mobile phone, I inquired into the features of the device, and what it symbolised for these users. Internet access, mobile banking and online media were mentioned in Ghana and India as among the 'services' that the mobile can offer, as one woman in Bihar explained: '*It can be used to call people who are far away or to use the internet. You can even read the newspaper on the mobile*'. These perceptions are often relayed by the advocates of mHealth, but they differ from the way mobiles are used in practice; rather, they reflect what people imagine mobiles can do. When the subject of actual usage is raised, it become clear that mobile services remain largely inaccessible to women. As another Bihari woman put it: '*Sometimes, there is no credit in the phone for two months. Only if there is an emergency and someone is going to market, I will ask her if she can top it up*'. As in Ghana, '*The benefits of the mobile are limited because call charges are too high to make access affordable*'.

In reality, almost all of the women interviewed in Ghana and Bihar use their mobiles only to receive calls. They never use text messages,[12] mobile internet or mobile banking services. They have very basic phones, not smartphones; they do not even have the kind of phone with simple internet access or music-listening features that are frequently found among the men in the same village. Nearly a quarter of the women with their own mobiles stated that they had defective devices, as one group of women in Bihar echoed: '"*I have my own mobile, but it doesn't work anymore.*" [Another woman in the group reacts] "*I also have a mobile that no longer works: the battery doesn't charge up any*

---

[12] In many cases due to illiteracy (50 per cent of women in Bihar and 45 per cent of women in rural Ghana), but also on account of the local languages not being commonly written (such as Fanté in Ghana) or of the women's cheap telephones being unable to display the Devanagari script for Hindi, the only writing system familiar to Bihari women who can read and write. See the figures from the Ghana Statistical Service: 'Fast Facts from the 2014 Ghana Demographic and Health Survey', and from the Government of India Census: 'Annual Health Survey – Bihar', 2012–13.

*more"'*. Where women do have a mobile, they are the most basic models, often faulty ones passed down by men who no longer want them. This systematic state of women being under-equipped (Tabet, 1979) is visible in both fieldwork areas and has been reported by other studies on mobile usage in sub-Saharan Africa (Porter *et al.*, 2012).

Gender inequalities are also found in spending on phone credit. In Ghana, where women represent more than 57 per cent of the active population (UN and Ghana Statistical Service, 2013), most of the women encountered were in paid work. However, women in rural Bihar receive no income for their agricultural labour.[13] In the Indian sample, women have very little (if any) phone credit; it is always topped up by their husbands or the male head of the household, and the differences in mobile spending are very significant. When a woman has her own mobile, she will typically have twenty times less phone credit than her husband, as a woman in Bihar explains: *'My husband always spends much more money on his mobile, 300 to 400 rupees a month [4 to 6 euros], while mine is topped up for 10 to 20 rupees a month [10-to-30-euro cents]'*. The women, moreover, very rarely top up the credit themselves. One woman in Bihar tells of how she depends on her husband for every top-up, even if he lives far from the village: *'I make a missed call using another mobile and he calls me back. Sometimes it takes 10 days, sometimes a month, for him to top up my mobile credit, but what can I do, I'm at a loss'*. Thus, even for those women who do have their own mobile phones, men control their use of it by means of the top-up charges.

Mobile usage also reveals inequalities of spatial mobility that seem to run counter to the promise of ubiquity embodied in the mobile phone. These inequalities have been identified throughout the world (Uteng and Cresswell, 2008) but are more in evidence in Bihar than in Ghana. Women in Bihari villages have very limited spatial mobility. They do not have the right to move around without good reason, and they rarely do so alone. The women are therefore unable to top up their minutes themselves, for reasons of mobility, as they would have to stray too far from home, as one woman in Bihar explains: *'You can't get phone top-ups here. You have to go Bikram for that [2–3 km away]. How could women go there?'*[14] The mobile phone, it emerges, is becoming a means to restrict women's mobility even more, as they can be

---

[13] Barely 10 per cent of women in Bihar are in paid employment. Agricultural work is often paid for at household level, with the male head of household receiving payment for all the labourers in the household, women and children included.

[14] The surveys in Ghana and Bihar were conducted in villages that were accessible by road but several kilometres from the nearest small town. There are therefore very few shops in these villages.

contacted without them having to leave their houses. Moreover, for husbands working far from home, the mobile phone is a way of maintaining a direct link with their wives, and a form of remote control, by keeping tabs on their phone credit. In the words of one Bihari woman, whose husband refuses to allow her any spare credit, so that he can control every call she makes: '*He tells me: why do you always want credit in advance on your mobile, when I can top it up every time you need to make a call*'.

Analysis of these women's mobile usage reveals very strong gender inequalities in terms of access to the mobile itself, to the features it offers and to telephone credit. It illustrates the extent to which the mobile phone can reinforce the direct power of men over women, embodying the male domination already in place. Running counter to the prevailing discourse about the apparent empowerment made possible by mobile telephony, this study shows how the mobile phone can limit women's autonomy still further. This analysis is further refined by comparing the two areas of implementation of the same mobile initiative. While the mobile phone is an instrument of male domination in India and Ghana alike, the gender inequalities it reveals depend on broader political, economic and social factors that vary significantly from one country to the other and which I will analyse in the following sub-section.

## 6.2 Situating Technological Intersectionality

Adopting gender as the dominant framework of analysis has proved pertinent for highlighting the male–female inequalities and the male domination at work in the Motech system. Moreover, it needs to be considered in articulation with other inequalities that play a major role in the way mHealth programmes have come to modify existing inequalities or generate new ones. The issue of intersectionality first arose in political movements, particularly in the United States in the feminist movements of the 1970s and the civil rights movements of the 1980s (Crenshaw, 1989; Jaunait and Chauvin, 2012). It refers to the situation of individuals who undergo multiple forms of domination, summed up by the triad of 'race, class and gender'. Whereas this political intersectionality tends to isolate and prioritise relations of domination within an arithmetical logic, in which one layer of domination is added on top of another, sociological intersectionality seeks to avoid this accretional vision in order to analyse the particular configurations and compensation phenomena that come into play at the intersection between different social relations (Establet and Baudelot, 1992). The sociological concept of intersectionality is of particular interest in its interface with 'standpoint theory', especially as reformulated by feminists working in postcolonial studies. Standpoint theory, or the theory of situated knowledge, employed by the American socialist feminists of the 1980s and 1990s, affirms that neutrality is impossible, that we always adopt a particular viewpoint, that is a cultural and political stance. The initial formulations of standpoint theory presented women as a marginalised and oppressed group, whose minority standpoint is relevant in and of itself for understanding the domination that the group suffers (Smith, 1990). Postcolonial feminists saw this as reproducing a Western standpoint, and consequently reformulated and enriched it (Harding, 2004). Women do not all share the same views, or the same political objectives, moral values or economic interests, and any analysis needs to identify and situate these different standpoints.

Taking up Sandra Harding's formulation and the sociological concept of intersectionality, Nira Yuval-Davis introduces and discusses the ways in which a situated intersectional analysis can help describe, and explain, different forms of social, economic, political and personal inequality that are simultaneous and enmeshed, and can incorporate other gazes with regard to these differentially located and situated inequalities (Yuval-Davis, 2015). The concept of situated intersectionality enables me to relate the perceptions of Ghanaian women and Indian women enrolled in the same technical platform and to shed light on the compensatory phenomena that can emerge from this technological intersectionality (Al Dahdah, 2019c). From micro to macro, from the individual to the political, I seek to study the different spheres in which the technological inequalities thrown up by Motech are produced. This study is not exhaustive; its aim is to bring into focus the main inequalities and forms of domination encountered in my fieldwork areas and how they articulate. I propose to develop two of them in the following sub-sections. The first looks at the interpersonal relationship between caregiver and patient and how it is affected by the technical platform. The second analyses the women's financial resources and the public maternal healthcare schemes that the platform both overlooks and at the same time makes necessary.

## 6.3 The Unequal Caregiver–Patient Relationship

The caregiver–patient relationship has already been recognised as highly unequal and as a source of symbolic and even physical violence, particularly in the countries chosen by Motech (d'Oliveira, Diniz and Schraiber, 2002; Jaffré and Sardan, 2003). This relationship plays a key role in subscription to Motech, as women can only join the programme through the intermediary of a health worker.

In Bihar, women have a relationship of trust but also of subordination with the CHWs (whether ASHAs or AWWs). The ASHAs receive an indemnity from the Health Ministry for the awareness-raising activities they organise among women in the villages. The AWWs answer not to the Health Ministry but to the national programme to fight child malnutrition in rural India.[15] They are paid to manage the community centre of their village, where children under six years of age are given a daily meal; they can also receive the same indemnities as the ASHAs if they promote awareness of the Indian government's maternal health programmes among the women of their village. Under the Motech programme, ASHAs and AWWs are in charge of persuading the women in their community to sign up to Kilkari. They are usually the only people to turn to on health matters in the villages, and most of the women encountered said that they had been a source of support during their pregnancy.[16] The women subscribe to Kilkari because their regular health worker advised them to. They join voluntarily, but do not always know what the service proposes or that it is a paid service, and that 1 rupee will be deducted from their phone credit for each voice message they listen to, as these verbatims illustrate: '*I asked her [the ASHA] why she wanted me to give her my mobile phone. She told me that this way she could sign me up for Kilkari'; 'I wasn't told that the money would be deducted'*. From the outset, as with any caregiver–patient relationship, the relationship between health workers and their patients is unequal, but Motech reinforces the economic inequality between them. The health workers are often the only women in the village to be paid for what they do, which gives them greater financial independence than the other women. The technical platform widens this divide still further, as Kilkari rewards health workers with phone credit for signing up women. This system of payment by phone credit creates friction in the relationship, as an ASHA explains: '*One woman told me: credit is taken from my mobile account and goes directly into your account'*. Even if the credit transferred is small,[17] it creates an imbalance between the women who have to spend credit in order to enrol, and the health workers who earn credit for enrolling them.

The women encountered in Ghana speak of difficult relationships with CHWs and, unlike in Bihar, do not share a relationship of trust with them. Ghana's

---

[15] Specifically, the ICDS (Integrated Child Development Services) scheme managed by the Ministry of Women and Child Development.

[16] Most of the young women encountered live in the village of their in-laws, with whom they often have a difficult relationship, and they tend not to have built up many attachments in the village. The ASHAs and AWWs act as relays, informing them about health centres and about vaccination of family planning campaigns, and accompanying pregnant women to appointments or for childbirth, for which they receive some payment. They are spontaneously cited by the women encountered as trustworthy people who helped them during their pregnancy. The interviews with the ASHAs and AWWs were conducted several days earlier and at several kilometres from the community centres where the interviews with the women were held, and therefore had no impact on the women's responses regarding their relationships with the ASHAs and AWWs.

[17] 10 rupees (0.13 euros) credit per subscription lasting at least four weeks, rising to 20 rupees after eight weeks.

'Community Health Officers' (CHOs), usually women, are nurses who have received six months training in community healthcare from the Ghana Ministry of Health. They are assigned to a community health centre where they live and provide primary healthcare services; in most cases they are not originally from the area. It is these nurses who were in charge of signing women up to Mobile Midwife as part of their awareness-raising mission. As the system is free of charge in Ghana, the women were often enrolled in Motech systematically simply as a result of attending the community health centre, as this woman explains: '*When I went for my antenatal visit, someone called me and told me I had been registered with Motech before I had even been told what it was about*'. Motech was presented to them as an integral part of the maternal healthcare regime, to which they were strongly advised to subscribe. None of the women encountered in Ghana spontaneously cited the CHOs as people who had counted during their pregnancy. Many of them have difficult relationships with these educated women from elsewhere who tell them how to behave 'properly' during their pregnancy. Moreover, the platform does enable some women to modify this hierarchical relationship: several speak of having a special relationship with the caregivers, thanks to Motech. Some state that subscribing to the platform allowed them to initiate a conversation and to raise questions to which the caregivers provided answers. The Motech messages seem, then, to have changed the relationship between the caregivers and the beneficiaries of the programme: '*I have the number of one of the midwives now. Without Motech, she would never have given it to me*'. And in the case of Ghana, Motech has smoothed the caregiver–patient relationship and enabled the women who subscribe to it to benefit from a more favourable status. In our interviews, the CHOs were perceived as more attentive and well-disposed towards the women enrolled in Motech, as the latter seek help from them more frequently after listening to the messages. However, this also implies that the platform, by its very presence, makes it still less likely for the other women to enjoy an easier relationship with the health professionals, an asymmetry which was criticised on several occasions by the women encountered: '*If you get the messages and you have problems, sometimes the nurses are more ready and willing to help you rather then help the ones that don't get the Motech messages*'. According to the interviewees, the non-Motech women have the impression that they take second place to the Motech women and are less well informed and/or treated.

The introduction of Motech disrupts the caregiver–patient relationship in India and in Ghana alike, but the inequalities are compensated or reinforced in different ways. In Bihar, the programme damages the relationship due to the financial imbalances that it generates. In Ghana, it sometimes improves a difficult relationship. However, while there may be an improvement for the women enrolled in the programme, it also runs the risk of detracting from that relationship for the women outside the programme, as voiced by the women encountered in Ghana.[18]

## 6.4 Disparities in Financial Resources and Access to Healthcare

The Motech system points up a variety of economic inequalities, underlining issues around the financial accessibility of the mobile service and of the health system in general. Financial resources are necessary first to acquire a mobile device and then to maintain it in operation, that is with sufficient charge and credit. The women are frequently dependent on men to obtain the money required, but the degree of difficulty involved is not the same for all of the women, as noted in the previous sub-section. The Ghanaian respondents, by virtue of their greater financial independence, can use their mobiles for work but also for the needs of their family, as they have the financial resources to cover the expenses incurred. They can consequently, to some extent, compensate for male domination and make financial decisions for the household, decisions that young Bihari women cannot make.[19]

The main mission of Motech is to encourage women to go to the health centre for monitoring and to give birth, but for them to do so involves substantial costs that are never mentioned in the messages. Access to healthcare in India and in Ghana is in large part paid for by households, and many respondents in India attested to the financial difficulties generated by maternal healthcare: '*I had to spend money for everything: medicines, injections, food. The nurses also asked me for money*'. Similarly in Ghana: '*the midwife should tell us how we are supposed to find the money to buy all the expensive things required by the maternity unit*'. The need for money is, for many women, the main barrier to being monitored by, or giving birth in, a health facility. Because the amount of money required for maternal healthcare is significant, it is usually met by men, even in the households where the women have their own income. Under the Motech system, the combined costs of healthcare and the mobile place conditions on access to health information and to healthcare, as a Ghanaian woman described: '*So if you don't have money to go to the health centre, you won't get the messages, because you won't be able to register for Motech. And if you do go, but you don't have a mobile – and not everyone does – you won't get the messages either*'. The programme therefore aggravates the women's financial distress and highlights their difficulties of access to health information and healthcare, without seeking to criticise this situation or compensate for it.

---

[18] The same phenomenon might have been observed in Bihar: if certain districts had been excluded from the scheme, the women in the districts not covered might have felt sidelined.

[19] In Bihar, the family purse strings are controlled by the men of the house or, in their absence, by older women, typically the mothers-in-law.

These financial difficulties are a primary reason for staying at home to give birth, and a major source of frustration with Motech, which encourages women to visit health facilities that they can often ill afford.

In South Asia, as in sub-Saharan Africa, the health sector reforms of the 1990s, along with structural adjustments, have brought about greater commercialisation of healthcare, through direct payment systems, increasing the out-of-pocket cost to patients (Kuhlmann and Annandale, 2010). Research shows that these reforms have had a disproportionate impact on access to maternal healthcare, with very significant increases in maternal mortality. These gender inequalities in financial access to the health system have been identified by numerous studies, leading to the implementation of compensatory policies for women. Both India and Ghana have recently introduced compensatory aid for maternal healthcare. Since 2008, in Ghana, access to maternal healthcare has been free of charge, thanks to the NHIS. My interviews suggest, however, that the scheme does not work well, and using the NHIS card to request free access to the health service can even lead to treatment being refused, as this woman explains: '*If you go through the NHIS system, the health professionals won't treat you, because it will take months for them to get the money for their work; they prefer to treat people who are ready to pay here and now*'. Several analyses confirm that the NHIS has not helped to improve maternal health, and has generated new inequalities of access to healthcare (Amporfu, 2013). In India, meanwhile, the national Janani Suraksha Yojana (JSY) programme, launched in 2005, aims to promote facility-based childbirth by providing compensatory payments for women. Targeting priority states such as Bihar, the programme offers a cheque for 1,400 rupees (20 euros) to women in rural areas who give birth at a health facility. Indeed, access to the programme remains complicated for many women, who do not always have the papers or the bank account required to benefit from it, and incur significant upfront costs to obtain it, as this woman attests: '*To be able to benefit from the 1,400-rupee (20 euros) aid payment, I have to have a bank account. To have an account, I must first put 500 rupees (7 euros) in it, before it can be opened. To open the account, I will need documents, and to obtain these documents I will have to pay baksheesh everywhere*'. Even after completing these eligibility requirements, some of the women still cannot obtain the money from the programme; they are told that the district has not received funds to proceed with the transfer: '*They say I will have to wait another two or three months, as there is no money left in the district coffers*'. In any case, the women feel that the scheme does not cover the costs of childbirth, let alone the costs of maternal healthcare. From transport to birth certificates, bribes or medicines, they have to pay out at every stage, to every professional and for every element of their care. In total, they spend the equivalent of at least 20–28 euros just to give birth, although their household income rarely exceeds 28 euros a month. Several analysts suggest that the JSY programme is inadequate, and that it generates significant financial and territorial inequalities (Centre for Equity Studies, 2015).

Public policies have been put in place to offset gender inequalities in access to care, but for both countries in the study they only very partially succeed in improving women's financial access to health facilities. These difficulties of access have a direct impact on the way the mHealth programmes are perceived. The Motech messages, by encouraging women to visit a health centre without mentioning or taking account of the associated financial barriers, lead to an additional form of symbolic violence for some women who, even if they wanted to go to the health centre, cannot do so, as one of them explains: '*What they say in the messages doesn't happen in reality; the facilities are not affordable, and I can't get a medical visit for me or my baby*'. Moreover, when the women do come to the health facilities, their experience is mostly negative: the staff are often absent, medicines and other health commodities have to be bought from the neighbouring market (Al Dahdah, Kumar and Quet, 2018) and they end up having to pay significant sums for treatments that are supposed to be free of charge.[20] As a Bihari woman told me: '*People go to the health centre because they think there are better infrastructures there than if they stayed at home to give birth. But in fact, there is no advantage in going there to give birth, and moreover it's too expensive*'.

This section shows that the Motech programme is conditioned by gendered relationships: access to and usage of mobile phones differ between men and women in the rural areas studied. The women in these villages are far less likely to own a mobile phone than the men. The situation is particularly exacerbated in Bihar, where most women have no income and therefore no financial independence. In this context, the mobile phone further reinforces existing patterns of male domination and confines women to the domestic space. Situated intersectionality allows for a more precise analysis of the inequalities that come into play in mHealth programmes, as it differentiates between unequal relationships in terms of the situations involved as well as the underlying intersections. For example, Motech opens up dialogue between caregivers and patients and thus improves the relationship a Ghanaian patient often finds difficult, whereas in Bihar it injects tension

---

[20] In Ghana and India, maternal care and childbirth in community health centres is free in theory but not, as my and others' research has shown, in practice.

into the caregiver–patient relationship due to the financial inequalities it generates between health workers and Bihari women. To imagine, as the designers of Motech suggest, that the weekly reception of a standardised voice message could uniformly redress such complex and varied inequalities as those found in this sociotechnical assemblage therefore seems utopian.

With health expenditure on the increase, public health policies (in North and South alike) place growing importance on individuals' personal responsibility for their own health, via the use of new technologies that facilitate access to health information (Harris, Wathen and Wyatt, 2010). mHealth is part of this development; 'patient accountability' is the core objective of Motech, drawing on behavioural theories employed for several decades to promote public health despite strong criticism from social scientists (Lupton, 2012). These behavioural programmes, past and present, do not seek to challenge systemic inequalities but serve above all to blame the individual and to absolve politicians of responsibility (Guérin, 2012). Analysis of the multiple inequalities at play in the Motech system demonstrates the limitations of the ideology of behavioural education in public health. By focusing on individual behaviours, programmes such as Motech overlook the barriers to healthcare access that result from a complex set of dynamics and determinants specific to a given health system. The geographic or financial accessibility of health facilities and the difficulties of caregiver–patient communication represent barriers that are hard to overcome, thwarting the initial Motech scenario in which the transmission of information would automatically lead to greater use of health services. By offering a technical solution thought to be neutral and universal, by focusing on people's personal responsibility for their own health and by ignoring the complex structure of social relations, the programme, by its very existence, consolidates pre-existing inequalities of gender and health.

## 7 Conclusion and Implications for Future Research

This Element shows how ideas, actors and targeted funding have managed to define a particular technology, that of the mobile telephone, as a relevant response to the challenges of development. The 'digital development' model promoted by mHealth initiatives reflects a convergence between development policies and the interests of telecoms players. As a prime example of this convergence, Motech is funded by the Gates Foundation and relies on a PPP between American and British private foundations and the Ghanaian and Indian health ministries. My work highlights the inequalities that characterise this type of partnership. In the case of Motech, on one side private actors from the Global North are very much in evidence, funding and steering the project, while on the other, governments from the Global South make their officials available but have no access in return to the technical platforms and databases enriched by their own teams. This Element demonstrates that such a division of tasks, unfavourable to the countries of the South, leads to deterioration in public health services by diverting vital human resources into projects of questionable utility. The private foundations present themselves as the only technical experts able to implement these innovative platforms, thereby blocking any transfer of technological knowledge and software skills and perpetuating North–South inequalities. For mHealth entrepreneurs in particular, the countries of the Global South are above all seen as untapped markets in which to invest.

## 7.1 mHealth as a Biomedical Technology

The present research also set out to understand how digital initiatives enmesh with healthcare practices. It shows that the use of digital technologies by patients and health professionals modifies biomedical practices at both the individual and collective levels. The Motech example reflects a determination to use digital technology to delegate certain aspects of healthcare to responsible patients and to health workers equipped with digital tools. The creation of 'responsible' patients relies mainly on automated health information systems which, via voice or text messages, remind individuals how they should act, and promote a behaviourist and consumerist vision of health. Additionally, this approach seeks to resolve the dysfunctions of health systems by leveraging Big Data – large data sets, indicators and algorithms generated by digital technology – to manage healthcare administration. My work highlights the unintended consequences of the 'datafication' of health when used for the purposes of managerial surveillance. Motech is sometimes employed to monitor the activities of health workers by tracking their use of mobile applications. These mechanisms pressurise already precarious and struggling workers and force them to perform additional administrative tasks instead of saving them time. Some administrators, moreover, encourage health workers to cut down on home visits to patients who are covered by Motech messages. I have also demonstrated that mHealth initiatives seeking to substitute digitised information for caregiver practice meet with significant resistance in the field and negatively impact the interpersonal relations that are so essential to healthcare. Health information, after all, is just one component of the healthcare process, which cannot be reduced to or entirely captured by digital encryption and transmission techniques. As this study shows, technologies that limit direct interaction between caregivers and patients, or between administrators and health workers, lead to a deterioration in healthcare and the health system.

Motech is one of a number of woman-centred development programmes that seek to compensate for gender inequalities by deploying methods and tools of empowerment. It illustrates the risk of reducing gender and the notion of empowerment to the individual mastery of techniques designed to reverse inequalities in favour of the oppressed. My research clearly shows, however, that mobile telephone usage in rural Ghana and Bihar is strongly gendered. Women, just as with other tools or technologies, are also under-equipped when it comes to mobile phones. These are primarily owned by men, and when the women do have one, they depend on men to top up their credit. The mobile can even reinforce pre-existing forms of male dominance and confine women still more closely to the home. However, the analysis does not stop at this observation: a comparative analysis shows how the Motech programme entrenches, amplifies or attenuates forms of domination and inequality in different ways in India and in Ghana. It shows, for example, the different ways in which the caregiver–patient relationship is transformed by the introduction of Motech. In Ghana, the women encountered describe difficult relationships with health workers, but Motech has to a certain degree improved the caregiver–patient relationship by making it less hierarchical. In India, where the women pay for access to Motech and where the health workers who enrol them are rewarded with phone credit, the platform tends instead to damage the caregiver–patient relationship, due to the financial imbalances it generates. These technical assemblages are conditioned by unequal relationships, but their presence, and the way they are used, modify these relationships in return.

The research summarised in this Element identifies the transformations brought about by digital technologies: at the international level, for the private actors of the Global North and the governments of the Global South; at the national level, for the health system and its employees; and finally at the local level, for the target population of women and the CHWs. It opens up a promising and currently under-researched field of study. mHealth is part of a more general movement towards globalisation and technologisation in biomedicine, which is embodied in a varied array of technical assemblages: eHealth, mHealth, telemedicine, Big Data and so on. This research invites new social science investigations to go beyond the case of mobile telephony to show how digital technologies are contributing to the emergence of new powers, the reconfiguration of roles, the growth of global digital assemblages, the datafication of health and the transformation of healthcare and health practices.

## 7.2 A Wealth of Digital Health Objects

While Motech is emblematic of the wave of mHealth projects in developing countries, it also illustrates a particular trend in mHealth in the Global South.

Motech offers an example of an mHealth project centred on the collection and transmission of health information. The investigation, however, touches on several lines of research that might usefully enable us to expand our focus. Firstly, within mHealth, other mechanisms are emerging which propose mobile health services that differ from Motech and are as yet unexplored. Secondly, to better understand the particular status that mHealth enjoys among recent developments in the biomedical field, we would need to document more widely the power issues at stake in digital health. Finally, digital health is itself one element in a much broader trend towards the digitalisation of practices of control and governmentality; to study this trend, we must extend our analysis to the political economy of digital in the Global South.

Among the many emerging mHealth phenomena, healthcare funding programmes constitute particularly interesting objects of study. For countries where the banking system remains weak, the possibility of coupling mHealth with mobile banking services (mMoney or mBanking) can help finance or make payments for healthcare provision using the money stored on a mobile phone (mHealth Alliance and World Economic Forum, 2011). The conjunction between mHealth and mBanking can then be used to provide micro-health insurance in countries without universal health coverage. In future work, I intend to focus on mHealth services that propose health coverage or a form of reimbursement of healthcare expenses based on telephone credit. Airtel Insurance, set up in Ghana at the beginning of 2014 by the Indian mobile operator Airtel, is an illustration of just such a phenomenon. This insurance scheme, which I discovered in Ghana, has since been rolled out to seven other countries in sub-Saharan Africa, including the key countries of Nigeria and Kenya. Its principle is simple: the operator Airtel rewards loyal customers by enabling them to sign up to 'free' health insurance provided they consume a certain amount of phone credit every month. The more the Airtel customer uses the operator's services, the better she is covered: '*Use more Airtel, get more insurance!*' The aim of this insurance mechanism is to act as a 'loss leader' to attract the many health service users in the Global South who have no health coverage and have to run up debts in order to pay for their health expenses. These initiatives amount to new objects of social protection to be analysed by future research, thereby helping to enrich our understanding of how mobile telephony is reshaping the landscape in terms of health and healthcare coverage.

The idea that digital technologies enable an improvement in patient care, a diminution in health disparities and an optimisation of health systems has in recent years been embodied in a varied array of technical assemblages: eHealth, mHealth, telemedicine, Big Data and so on. mHealth is one specific vector of this global movement. This research invites us to look beyond the case of mobile telephony to reveal how digital technologies are contributing to the emergence of new powers, the reconfiguration of roles, the growth of global digital assemblages, the datafication of health and the transformation of health-care and health practices. Further research is required in order to understand the rationale behind this broader movement of which mHealth is a part. To this end, it would be useful to compare mHealth with other digital health trends in the Global South, such as telemedicine (Duclos, 2014) or the health-related use of social media. The modalities and forms adopted by connected health in the Global South remain a field to be explored, and the governmentality of digital health a new assemblage to be examined.

## 7.3 The Political Economy of Digital in the Global South

In conclusion, this Element is based on the idea that the Global South is a key space of experimentation and development for digital technologies, which opens up a still wider field of study: that of the political economy of digital and the digital dissemination of political power in the Global South. A political economy of this kind would need to be analysed from three angles:

- Digital technologies are specific instruments for governing populations and people's lives. They are used to act upon and order the social through dynamics that combine technological developments with political projects (Agamben, 1997, Pestre, 2016, Rose and Novas, 2003) and must therefore be studied in a way that is attentive to the forms of governmentality involved in digital initiatives;
- Digital technologies are a factor in the renewal of the forms adopted by what Kaushik Sunder Rajan calls 'biocapital', which emerges from the encounter between the biomedical sciences and contemporary strategies of capital accumulation. Digital, as one of the current drivers of capitalism, gives a particular meaning to 'biocapitalism', which calls for a study designed to describe the interactions between communication technologies, commercial strategies and the production of knowledge (Rajan, 2012);
- Digital technologies are always situated in specific social, political and material landscapes (Harding, 2004) and must therefore be analysed in the light of the specificities of these contexts.

Seen from this triple approach, the countries of the South are sites of key importance in the deployment of the political economy of digital. The digital technologies being implemented there are renegotiating the frontiers between 'high tech' and 'low tech' that have traditionally separated the rich world from the rest. They are underpinned by particular political projects and reflect particular conceptions about the relationship between science, technology and society. They also mobilise particular national sociotechnical imaginaries (Jasanoff and Kim, 2009, 120) in a postcolonial context, embedded in and reacting to a long history of relations between societies, states and imperial powers. Digital policies in sub-Saharan Africa or in South Asia are helping to transform the vision that the world has of these 'less-developed' regions, which are appropriating, transforming and creating digital artefacts. The Indian government, for example, proposes to fight corruption by adopting e-governance, and to dematerialise social aid by implementing the world's largest biomedical database (Abraham and Rajadhyaksha, 2015), thereby redefining citizenship, social protection and resident rights in what will soon be the world's most populous country. Sub-Saharan Africa, meanwhile, is taking the digital hub route: Kenya's 'Silicon Savannah' is bringing together investors, engineers and developers to create tomorrow's 'Made in Africa' digital technologies (Park and Donovan, 2016). The objects and programmes developed in this context invite us to rethink innovation and the relationship between technology and society.

These three angles of analysis, combining approaches from the Sociology of Health and the Sociology of Science and Technology, form the outlines of a promising research agenda on the governmentality of digital technologies in the countries of the South, their usages, their integration into national or transnational policies and the power relations that emerge from these specific configurations.

# Abbreviations

| Abbreviation | Meaning |
| --- | --- |
| ASHA | Accredited Social Health Activist |
| AWW | Anganwadi Worker |
| BCM | Block community manager |
| BMGF | The Bill & Melinda Gates Foundation |
| CHO | Community health officers |
| CHPS | Community Health Planning & Services |
| CHW | Community health worker |
| FLW | Frontline workers |
| GHS | Ghana Health Service |
| GPRS | General Packet Radio Service |
| ICT | Information and communication technologies |
| JSY | Janani Suraksha Yojana |
| LDC | Least developed countries |
| MDG | Millennium Development Goals |
| mBanking | Mobile banking services |
| MCTS | Mother and Child Tracking System |
| mForms | Mobile data forms |
| mHealth | Mobile health |
| mMoney | Mobile money |
| Motech | Mobile Technology for Community Health |
| NGA | National Geospatial-Intelligence Agency |
| NHIS | National Health Insurance Scheme |
| PPP | Public–private partnership |
| QS | Quantified self |
| SIM | Subscriber Identification Module |
| SMS | Text Messaging Service |
| STS | Science and Technology Studies |

# References

Abraham, I. and Rajadhyaksha, A. (2015) 'State power and technological citizenship in India: From the postcolonial to the digital age', *East Asian Science, Technology and Society*, 9(1), pp. 65–85. https://doi.org/10.1215/18752160-2863200.

Adams, V., Novotny, T. E. and Leslie, H. (2008) 'Global health diplomacy', *Medical Anthropology*, 27(4), pp. 315–23. https://doi.org/10.1080/01459740802427067.

Agamben, Giorgio, et Marilène Raiola (1997). *Homo Sacer : Le pouvoir souverain et la vie nue*. Paris: Seuil.

Akrich, M. *et al.* (2006) *Sociologie de la traduction: textes fondateurs*. Paris: Mines Paris, les Presses.

Akrich, M. (2010) 'Comment décrire les objets techniques?', *Techniques & Culture. Revue semestrielle d'anthropologie des techniques*, (54–55), pp. 205–19. https://doi.org/10.4000/tc.4999.

Akrich, M. and Méadel, C. (2007) 'De l'interaction à l'engagement : les collectifs électroniques, nouveaux militants dans le champ de la santé', *Hermès*, (47), pp. 145–54.

Akrich, M. and Méadel, C. (2010) 'Internet, tiers nébuleux de la relation patient-médecin', *Les Tribunes de la santé*, 29(4), p. 41. https://doi.org/10.3917/seve.029.0041.

Al Dahdah, M., Du Loû A. D. and Méadel C. (2015) *Health Policy and Technology*, 4 (3), 225–31.

Al Dahdah, M. (2019a) 'Between philanthropy and big business: The rise of mHealth in the global health market', *Development and Change* [Preprint], 53, pp. 376–95. https://doi.org/10.1111/dech.12497.

Al Dahdah, M. (2019b) 'Les mobiles du développement : le téléphone portable comme outil d'empowerment des femmes des Suds?', *Terminal. Technologie de l'information, culture & société* [Preprint], (125–126). https://doi.org/10.4000/terminal.5013.

Al Dahdah, M. (2019c) 'La santé maternelle par téléphone portable au Ghana et en Inde : inégalités et intersections technologiques', *Critique internationale*, 83(2), pp. 147–66.

Al Dahdah, M. and Kumar, A. (2018). 'Mobile phones for maternal health in rural Bihar reducing the access gap?' *Economic and Political Weekly* 53, 11 (2018), pp. 50–7.

Al Dahdah, M. and Kumar, A. (2021) 'Digitalizing community health: Mobile phones to improve maternal health in rural India', in Jullien, C. and Jeffery, R. (eds) *Childbirth in South Asia: Old challenges and new paradoxes*. Oxford: Oxford University Press, pp. 308–26.

Al Dahdah, M., Kumar, A. and Quet, M. (2018) 'Empty stocks and loose paper: Governing access to medicines through informality in Northern India', *International Sociology*, 33(6), p. 18. https://doi.org/Ds:O//dIo:i1.o0r.g1/ 107.171/0772/6082568508901981787992779.

Al Dahdah, M. and Quet, M. (2020) 'Between tech and trade, the digital turn in development policies', *Development*, 63, pp. 219–25. https://doi.org/ 10.1057/s41301-020-00272-y

Alepis, E. and Lambrinidis, C. (2013) 'M-health: Supporting automated diagnosis and electonic health records', *SpringerPlus*, 2(1), p. 103. https://doi .org/10.1186/2193-1801-2-103.

Amporfu, E. (2013) 'Equity of the premium of the Ghanaian national health insurance scheme and the implications for achieving universal coverage', *International Journal for Equity in Health*, 12(4), pp. 4–9. www.biomed central.com/content/pdf/1475-9276-12-4.pdf (Accessed: 22 January 2015).

Anderson, W. (2009) 'From subjugated knowledge to conjugated subjects: Science and globalisation, or postcolonial studies of science?', *Postcolonial Studies*, 12(4), pp. 389–400. https://doi.org/10.1080/ 13688790903350641.

Arnold, D. (2000) *Science, technology and medicine in colonial India*. Cambridge: Cambridge University Press.

Arvanitis, R. *et al.* (2008) 'Sciences, savoirs et mondialisations', *M.U.R.S, Paris* [Preprint]. http://documents.irevues.inist.fr/bitstream/handle/2042/ 25037/sdh_2008_57-58_48.pdf?sequence=1 (Accessed: 8 April 2013).

Bajwa, M. I. (2014) 'mHealth security', *Pakistan Journal of Medical Sciences*, 30(4), pp. 904–907. https://doi.org/10.12669/pjms.304.5210.

Bashir Ahmad Bhat (2015) 'A study of involvment of men in reproductive health in J&K – India', in Sharma, S. (ed.) *Maternal and child health in India: policies and challenges*. Delhi, India: Bookwell, pp. 125–38.

Bennett, C. J. (2011) 'In defense of privacy: The concept and the regime', *Surveillance & Society*, 8(4), pp. 485–96.

Bijker, W. E. and Law, J. (1992) *Shaping technology/building society: Studies in sociotechnical change*. Cambridge, MA: MIT Press.

Blumenstock, J. E. (2012) 'Inferring patterns of internal migration from mobile phone call records: Evidence from Rwanda', *Information Technology for Development*, 18(2), pp. 107–25.

Boyd, D. and Crawford, K. (2012) 'Critical questions for big data: Provocations for a cultural, technological, and scholarly phenomenon', *Information, Communication & Society*, 15(5), pp. 662–79. https://doi.org/10.1080/1369118X.2012.678878.

Brukum, N. J. K. (1985) *Afro-European Relations on the Gold Coast, 1791–1844*. M.A. thesis, Legon: University of Ghana.

Callaway, D. W. *et al.* (2012) 'Disaster mobile health technology: lessons from Haiti', *Prehospital and Disaster Medicine*, 27(2), pp. 148–52. https://doi.org/10.1017/S1049023X12000441.

Calvès, A.-E. (2009) '« Empowerment » : généalogie d'un concept clé du discours contemporain sur le développement', *Tiers-Monde*, 200(4), p. 735. https://doi.org/10.3917/rtm.200.0735.

Cardon, D. (2015) *A quoi rêvent les algorithmes: Nos vies à l'heure des big data*. Paris: Seuil.

Case, T., Morrison, C. and Vuylsteke, A. (2012) 'The clinical application of mobile technology to disaster medicine', *Prehospital and Disaster Medicine*, 27(5), pp. 473–80. https://doi.org/10.1017/S1049023X12001173.

Cassier, M. (2002) 'Propriété industrielle et santé publique', *Projet*, 270(2), p. 47. https://doi.org/10.3917/pro.270.0047.

Centre for Equity Studies (2015) *Broken lives and compromise. Report on maternity entitlement in India*. http://centreforequitystudies.org/wp-content/uploads/2015/06/Maternity-Entitlement-Report_CES_29.05.pdf (Accessed: 29 January 2016).

Chéneau-Loquay (2012) 'La téléphonie mobile dans les villes africaines. Une adaptation réussie au contexte local', *EG Espace Géographique*, 41(1), p. 96.

Chib, A. (2010) 'The Aceh Besar midwives with mobile phones project: Design and evaluation perspectives using the information and communication technologies for healthcare development model', *Journal of Computer-Mediated Communication*, 15(3), pp. 500–25. https://doi.org/10.1111/j.1083-6101.2010.01515.x.

Chib, A., van Velthoven, M. H. and Car, J. (2015) 'mHealth adoption in low-resource environments: A review of the use of mobile healthcare in developing countries', *Journal of Health Communication*, 20(1), pp. 4–34. https://doi.org/10.1080/10810730.2013.864735.

Clarke, R. (1988) 'Information technology and dataveillance', *Communications of the ACM*, 31(5), pp. 498–512.

Cocosila, M. and Archer, N. (2005) 'A framework for mobile healthcare answers to chronically ill outpatient non-adherence', *Informatics in Primary Care*, 13(2), pp. 145–52.

Conein, B., Dodier, N. and Thévenot, L. (1993) 'Les objets dans l'action', *Raisons Pratiques* [Preprint]. http://cat.inist.fr/?aModele=afficheN&cpsidt=61716 (Accessed: 9 February 2016).

Crampton, J. W., Roberts, S. M. and Poorthuis, A. (2014) 'The new political economy of geographical intelligence', *Annals of the Association of American Geographers*, 104(1), pp. 196–214. https://doi.org/10.1080/00045608.2013.843436.

Crenshaw, K. (1989) 'Demarginalizing the intersection of race and sex: A black feminist critique of antidiscrimination doctrine, feminist theory and antiracist politics', *The University of Chicago Legal Forum*, 140, pp. 139–67.

Dagiral, E. and Parasie, S. (2015) 'La « science des données » à la conquête des mondes sociaux. Ce que le « Big Data » doit aux épistémologies locales', in Menger, P.-M. and Paye, S. (eds) *Big Data, entreprises à paraître en 2015 et sciences sociales*. Paris: Editions du Collège de France, pp. 85–104.

d'Oliveira, A. F. P. L., Diniz, S. G. and Schraiber, L. B. (2002) 'Violence against women in health-care institutions: an emerging problem', *The Lancet*, 359 (9318), pp. 1681–85.

Donovan, K. and Martin, A. (2012) *The Rise of African SIM Registration: The Emerging Dynamics of Regulatory Change*. SSRN Scholarly Paper ID 2172283. Rochester: Social Science Research Network. https://doi.org/10.2139/ssrn.2172283.

Duclos, V. (2014) *Le soin du monde: Incursions anthropologiques dans le Pan-African e-Network project*. https://papyrus.bib.umontreal.ca/xmlui/handle/1866/10788 (Accessed: 16 September 2014).

Edgerton, D. (1998) 'De l'innovation aux usages. Dix thèses éclectiques sur l'histoire des techniques', *Annales. Histoire, Sciences Sociales*. Translated by D. Pestre, 53(4), pp. 815–37. https://doi.org/10.3406/ahess.1998.279700.

Epstein, S. (2007) *Inclusion: The politics of difference in medical research*. Chicago: University of Chicago Press (Chicago studies in practices of meaning).

Erikson, S. L. (2018) 'Cell phones ≠ self and other problems with big data detection and containment during epidemics: Problems with big data detection and containment', *Medical Anthropology Quarterly* [Preprint], 32(3), pp.315–39. https://doi.org/10.1111/maq.12440.

Establet, R. and Baudelot, C. (1992) *Allez les filles*. Paris: Editions du Seuil.

European Union Commission (2014) *Green paper on mobile health ('mHealth')*. Brussels. https://ec.europa.eu/digital-agenda/en/news/green-paper-mobile-health-mhealth (Accessed: 13 April 2014).

Fassin, D. (2006) *Quand les corps se souviennent: Expériences et politiques du sida en Afrique du Sud*. Paris: La Découverte (Armillaire).

Federal Trade Commission (2013) *Mobile privacy disclosures.* www.ftc.gov/news-events/press-releases/2013/02/ftc-staff-report-recommends-ways-improve-mobile-privacy (Accessed: 22 January 2014).

Fischer, M. M. (2003) *Emergent forms of life and the anthropological voice.* Durham: Duke University Press.

Flichy, P. (2003) *L'innovation technique: Récents développements en sciences sociales, vers une nouvelle théorie de l'innovation.* Nouv. éd. Paris: La Découverte (Sciences et société).

Gardey, D. (2003) 'De la domination a l'action: Quel genre d'usage des technologies de l'information?' *Réseaux*, 120(4), p. 87. https://doi.org/10.3917/res.120.0087.

Gaudillière, J.-P. (2002) *Inventer la biomédecine: la France, l'Amérique et la production des savoirs du vivant, 1945–1965.* Paris: La Découverte (Textes à l'appui).

Gaudillière, J.-P. *et al.* (2020) *Global health and the new world order: Historical and anthropological approaches to a changing regime of governance.* Manchester: Manchester University Press.

Gitelman, L. (ed.) (2013) *'Raw data' is an oxymoron.* Cambridge: The MIT Press (Infrastructures series).

Grameen Foundation (2012) *MOTECH lessons learned.* https://grameenfoundation.org/resource/motech-lessons-learned (Accessed: 8 October 2013).

Greenleaf, G. (2014) 'Sheherezade and the 101 data privacy laws: Origins, significance and global trajectories', *JL Inf. & Sci.*, 23, p. 4.

GSMA (2013) *Women & mobile: A global opportunity. A study on the mobile phone gender gap in low and middle-income countries.* www.gsma.com/mobilefordevelopment/wp-content/uploads/2013/01/GSMA_Women_and_Mobile-A_Global_Opportunity.pdf (Accessed: 3 February 2014).

Guérin, I. (2012) 'L'éducation financière ou comment apprendre aux pauvres à bien consommer', in Guérin, I. and Sélim, M. (eds) *À quoi et comment dépenser son argent?: hommes et femmes face aux mutations globales de la consommation.* Paris: L'Harmattan, pp. 51–71.

Gurumurthy, A. (2004) 'Combattre les inégalités de genre dans la société d'information', *Genre et développement, En Bref, Genre et TIC* [Preprint], (15). www.bridge.ids.ac.uk/Docs/enbref15.pdf (Accessed: 4 April 2013).

Haggerty, R. V. and Ericson, K. (2000) 'The surveillant assemblage', *British Journal of Sociology*, 51(4), pp. 605–22. https://doi.org/10.1080/00071310020015280.

Haraway, D. J. *et al.* (2007) *Manifeste cyborg et autres essais: Sciences, fictions, féminismes.* Paris: Exils (Essais).

Harding, S. G. (ed.) (2004) *The feminist standpoint theory reader: Intellectual and political controversies*. New York: Routledge.

Harris, R. M., Wathen, C. N. and Wyatt, S. (2010) *Configuring health consumers health work and the imperative of personal responsibility*. New York: Palgrave Macmillan. http://public.eblib.com/choice/publicfullrecord.aspx?p=652305 (Accessed: 3 July 2016).

Harvey, M. J. and Harvey, M. G. (2014) 'Privacy and security issues for mobile health platforms: Privacy and security issues for mobile health platforms', *Journal of the Association for Information Science and Technology*, 65(7), pp. 1305–18. https://doi.org/10.1002/asi.23066.

Henwood, F. and Wyatt, S. (2000) 'Persistent inequalities?: Gender and technology in the year 2000', *Feminist Review, No. 64, Feminism 2000: One Step beyond?*, 64, pp. 128–31 Published by: Palgrave Macmillan Journals.

ITU (2013) *The world in 2013 : ICT facts and figures*. www.itu.int/en/ITU-D/Statistics/Documents/facts/ICTFactsFigures2013.pdf (Accessed: 5 April 2013).

ITU (2014) *World in 2014 : ICT facts and figures*. www.itu.int/en/ITU-D/Statistics/Documents/facts/ICTFactsFigures2014-e.pdf (Accessed: 13 May 2014).

ITU (2019) *Measuring digital development : Facts and figures 2019*. Geneva: ITU.

ITU and UNESCO (2013) *Doubling digital opportunities : Enhancing the inclusion of women and girls in the information society*. Genève: UNDP. www.broadbandcommission.org/Documents/working-groups/bb-doubling-digital-2013.pdf (Accessed: 6 November 2013).

Jaffré, Y. and Sardan, J.-P. O. de (eds) (2003) *Une médecine inhospitalière: les difficiles relations entre soignants et soignés dans cinq capitales d'Afrique de l'Ouest*. Paris: Karthala [u.a.] (Hommes et sociétés).

Jasanoff, S. (2005) *Designs on nature*. London: Princeton University Press.

Jasanoff, S. and Kim, S.-H. (2009) 'Containing the atom: Sociotechnical imaginaries and nuclear power in the United States and South Korea', *Minerva*, 47(2), pp. 119–46.

Jaunait, A. and Chauvin, S. (2012) 'Représenter l'intersection: Les théories de l'intersectionnalité à l'épreuve des sciences sociales', *Revue française de science politique*, 62(1), p. 5. https://doi.org/10.3917/rfsp.621.0005.

Jerven, M. (2013) *Poor numbers: How we are misled by African development statistics and what to do about it*. New York: Cornell University Press.

Joly, P.-B., Rip, A. and Callon, M. (2013) 'Réinventer l'innovation?' http://webcom.upmf-grenoble.fr/lodel/innovacs/index.php?id=108#tocto1n3 (Accessed: 23 January 2014).

Jouët, J. (2000) 'Retour critique sur la sociologie des usages', *Réseaux*, 18(100), pp. 487–521. https://doi.org/10.3406/reso.2000.2235.

Kaewkungwal, J. *et al.* (2010) 'Application of smart phone in "better border healthcare program": A module for mother and child care', *BMC Medical Informatics and Decision Making*, 10(1), p. 69. https://doi.org/10.1186/1472-6947-10-69.

Källander, K. *et al.* (2013) 'Mobile health (mHealth) approaches and lessons for increased performance and retention of community health workers in low- and middle-income countries: a review', *Journal of Medical Internet Research*, 15(1), p. e17. https://doi.org/10.2196/jmir.2130.

Kuhlmann, E. and Annandale, E. (eds) (2010) *The Palgrave handbook of gender and healthcare*. Basingstoke: Palgrave Macmillan.

de Laet, M. and Mol, A. (2000) 'The Zimbabwe bush pump: Mechanics of a fluid technology', *Social Studies of Science*, 30(2), pp. 225–63. https://doi.org/10.1177/030631200030002002.

Lester, R. T. *et al.* (2010) 'Effects of a mobile phone short message service on antiretroviral treatment adherence in Kenya (WelTel Kenya1): a randomised trial', *The Lancet*, 376(9755), pp. 1838–45. https://doi.org/10.1016/S0140-6736(10)61997-6.

Lupton, D. (2012) 'M-health and health promotion: The digital cyborg and surveillance society', *Social Theory & Health*, 10(3), pp. 229–44.

Lupton, D. (2013) 'Quantifying the body: monitoring and measuring health in the age of mHealth technologies', *Critical Public Health*, 23(4), pp. 393–403. https://doi.org/10.1080/09581596.2013.794931.

Lupton, D. and Jutel, A. (2015) '"It's like having a physician in your pocket!" A critical analysis of self-diagnosis smartphone apps', *Social Science & Medicine*, 133, pp. 128–35. https://doi.org/10.1016/j.socscimed.2015.04.004.

Lyon, D. (2011) 'Surveillance, Power and Everyday Life', in Kalantzis-Cope, P. and Gherab Martín, K. (eds) *Emerging digital spaces in contemporary society properties of technology*. Basingstoke: Palgrave Macmillan. http://lib.myilibrary.com?id=299925 (Accessed: 21 September 2015).

Lyon, D. (2014) 'Surveillance, snowden, and big data: Capacities, consequences, critique', *Big Data & Society*, 1(2). https://doi.org/10.1177/2053951714541861.

MacKenzie, D. A. and Wajcman, J. (1999) *The social shaping of technology*. 2nd ed. Buckingham [Eng.]; Philadelphia: Open University Press.

Mahajan, M. (2019) 'The IHME in the shifting landscape of global health metrics', *Global Policy*, 10(S1), pp. 110–20. https://doi.org/10.1111/1758-5899.12605.

Mahmud, N., Rodriguez, J. and Nesbit, J. (2010) 'A text message-based intervention to bridge the healthcare communication gap in the rural developing world', *Technology and Health Care: Official Journal of the European Society for Engineering and Medicine*, 18(2), pp. 137–44. https://doi.org/10.3233/THC-2010-0576.

Mansell, R. (2011) 'Technology, innovation, power and social consequence', in Kalantzis-Cope, P. and Gherab Martín, K. (eds) *Emerging digital spaces in contemporary society properties of technology.* Basingstoke: Palgrave Macmillan, pp. 13–25. http://lib.myilibrary.com?id=299925 (Accessed: 21 September 2015).

Marcus, G. E. (1995) 'Ethnography in/of the world system: the emergence of multi-sited ethnography', *Annual Review of Anthropology*, 24(1), pp. 95–117.

Massey, T. and Gao, T. (2010) 'Mobile health systems that optimize resources in emergency response situations', in *AMIA Annual Symposium Proceedings*, p. 502. www.ncbi.nlm.nih.gov/pmc/articles/PMC3041325/ (Accessed: 9 December 2013).

mHealth Alliance (2012) *Advancing the dialogue on mobile finance and mobile health: Country case studies.* www.mhealthknowledge.org/sites/default/files/23_advancing_the_dialogue.mhealth_alliance.pdf.

mHealth Alliance and UN Foundation (2013) *State of evidence: mHealth and MNCH.Trends, gaps, stakeholder needs, and opportunities for future research on the use of mobile technology to improve maternal, newborn, and child health.* http://mhealthalliance.org/images/content/un_007_eviden cegapreport_digital_aaa.pdf (Accessed: 18 December 2013).

mHealth Alliance and World Economic Forum (2011) *Amplifying the impact: Examining the intersection of mobile health and mobile finance.* www.mhealthknowledge.org/resources/amplifying-impact-examining-intersec tion-mobile-health-and-mobile-finance.

Neff, G. (2013) 'Why big data won't cure us', *big data*, 1(3), pp. 117–23. https://doi.org/10.1089/big.2013.0029.

Noordam, A. C. *et al.* (2011) 'Improvement of maternal health services through the use of mobile phones', *Tropical Medicine & International Health*, 16(5), pp. 622–6. https://doi.org/10.1111/j.1365-3156.2011.02747.x.

Ntsua, S. *et al.* (2012) *Repositioning community-based family planning in Ghana: A case study of community-based health planning and services (CHPS).* Washington, DC: The Population Council. www.popcouncil.org/uploads/pdfs/2012PGY_CaseStudyCHPS.pdf (Accessed: 25 March 2014).

Ollion, É. and Boelaert, J. (2015) 'Au delà des big data. Les sciences sociales et la multiplication des données numériques', *Sociologie*, 6(3), pp. 295–310.

Ong, A. and Collier, S. J. (2005) *Global assemblages: technology, politics, and ethics as anthropological problems*. Malden, MA: Blackwell.

Oudshoorn, N. (2011) *Telecare technologies and the transformation of health-care*. New York: Palgrave Macmillan (Health, technology and society).

Park, E. and Donovan, K. (2016) 'Between the nation and the state', *Limn*, 9 August. http://limn.it/between-the-nation-and-the-state/ (Accessed: 23 September 2016).

Parpart, J. L. *et al.* (2003) *Rethinking empowerment gender and development in a global/local world*. New York: Routledge. http://public.eblib.com/choice/publicfullrecord.aspx?p=171259 (Accessed: 21 January 2016).

Pestre, D. (2016) *Le gouvernement des technosciences: Gouverner le progrès et ses dégâts depuis 1945*. Paris: La Découverte.

Petitjean, P., Jami, C. and Moulin, A.-M. (eds) (1992) *Science and empires historical studies about scientific development and European expansion*. Dordrecht: Springer Netherlands. http://public.eblib.com/choice/PublicFullRecord.aspx?p=3070741 (Accessed: 24 October 2016).

Porter, G. *et al.* (2012) 'Youth, mobility and mobile phones in Africa: Findings from a three-country study', *Information Technology for Development*, 18(2), pp. 145–62. https://doi.org/10.1080/02681102.2011.643210.

Potvin, L. and Frohlich, K. L. (1998) 'L'utilité de la notion de genre pour comprendre les inégalités de santé entre les hommes et les femmes', *Ruptures-Montreal-*, 5, pp. 142–52.

Proulx, S. (2005) 'Penser les usages des technologies de l'information et de la communication aujourd'hui : enjeux – modèles – tendances', in Lise Vieira et Nathalie Pinède (ed.) *Enjeux et usages des TIC : aspects sociaux et culturels*. Paris: Presses universitaires de Bordeaux, pp. 7–20.

Quet, M. (2012) 'La critique des technologies émergentes face à la communication prometteuse. Contestations autour des nanotechnologies', *Réseaux*, 173–4(3), p. 271. https://doi.org/10.3917/res.173.0271.

Rajan, K. S. (2008) 'Biocapital as an emergent form of life', in Gibbon, S. and Novas, C. (eds) *Biosocialities, genetics and the social sciences: Making biologies and identities*. New York: Routledge, pp. 157–87.

Rajan, K. S. (2012) *Lively capital: biotechnologies, ethics, and governance in global markets*. Durham: Duke University Press.

Raley, R. (2013) 'Dataveillance and countervailance', in Gitelman, L. (ed.) *'Raw data' is an oxymoron*. Cambridge: The MIT Press, pp. 121–145.

Ramachandran, D., Goswami, V. and Canny, J. (2010) ' Research and reality: - using mobile messages to promote maternal health in rural India'. In *Proceedings of the 4th ACM/IEEE international conference on information and communication technologies and development* (pp. 1–10).

Ribes, D. and Jackson, S. (2013) 'Data bite man: The work of sustaining a long-term study', in Gitelman, L. (ed.) *'Raw data' is an oxymoron*. Cambridge: The MIT Press (Infrastructures series), pp. 147–66.

Ronsmans, C. and Graham, W. J. (2006) 'Maternal mortality: who, when, where, and why', *The Lancet*, 368(9542), pp. 1189–200. https://doi.org/10.1016/S0140-6736(06)69380-X.

Rose, Nikolas, et Carlos Novas (2003). « Biological Citizenship ». In *Aihwa Ong and Stephen Collier (*eds.) *Global Anthropology*. Blackwell.

Sachs, Jeffrey (2018). « The digital war on poverty ». *The Guardian*. http://www.theguardian.com/commentisfree/2008/aug/21/digitalmedia.mobilephones.

Sankaranarayanan, J. and Sallach, R. E. (2013) '"Rural patients" access to mobile phones and willingness to receive mobile phone-based pharmacy and other health technology services: A pilot study', *Telemedicine Journal and e-Health: The Official Journal of the American Telemedicine Association* [Preprint], pp. 182–85. https://doi.org/10.1089/tmj.2013.0150.

Sardenberg, C. (2008) 'Liberal vs. liberating empowerment: A Latin American feminist perspective on conceptualising women's empowerment', *IDS Bulletin*, 39(6), pp. 18–27.

Sawadogo, N. H., Sanou, H., Greene, J. A. and Duclos, V. (2021) « Promises and perils of mobile health in Burkina Faso ». *The Lancet*, 398(10302), 738–39.

Servet, J.-M. (2015) 'L'économisme rampant de la « nouvelle » économie comportementale. Une lecture critique du World Development Report 2015 de la Banque mondiale'. www.veblen-institute.org/IMG/pdf/jm_servet_epargne_et_monnaie.pdf (Accessed: 11 January 2016).

Shrum, W. (2000) 'Science and story in development: The emergence of non-governmental organizations in agricultural research', *Social Studies of Science*, 30(1), pp. 95–124. https://doi.org/10.1177/030631200030001004.

Sim, S. E. and Philip, K. (2008) 'Tracing transnational flows of IT knowledge through open exchange of software development know-how'. www.ideals.illinois.edu/handle/2142/15075 (Accessed: 28 April 2014).

Smith, D. E. (1990) *The conceptual practices of power: A feminist sociology of knowledge*. Toronto: University of Toronto Press.

Stoner, S. A. and Hendershot, C. S. (2012) 'A randomized trial evaluating an mHealth system to monitor and enhance adherence to pharmacotherapy for alcohol use disorders', *Addiction Science & Clinical Practice*, 7(1), p. 9. https://doi.org/10.1186/1940-0640-7-9.

Suchman, L. (2008) 'Feminist STS and the sciences of the artificial', in Society for Social Studies of Science (ed.) *The handbook of science and technology studies*. 3rd ed. Cambridge, MA: MIT Press; Published in cooperation with the Society for the Social Studies of Science, pp. 139–64.

Tabet, P. (1979) 'Les Mains, les outils, les armes', *L'Homme*, 19(3), pp. 5–61. doi:10.3406/hom.1979.367998.

Tamrat, T. and Kachnowski, S. (2011) 'Special delivery: An analysis of mHealth in maternal and newborn health programs and their outcomes around the world', *Maternal and Child Health Journal*, 16(5), pp. 1092–101. doi:10.1007/s10995-011-0836-3.

Taylor, L. (2015) 'No place to hide? The ethics and analytics of tracking mobility using mobile phone data', *Environment and Planning D: Society and Space*, 34, pp. 319–36.

Taylor, L. and Schroeder, R. (2015) 'Is bigger better? The emergence of big data as a tool for international development policy', *GeoJournal*, 80(4), pp. 503–18. https://doi.org/10.1007/s10708-014-9603-5.

Tsing, A. L. (2005) *Friction: an ethnography of global connection*. Princeton: Princeton University Press.

Uimonen, P. (2016) '"Number not reachable" : Mobile infrastructure and global racial hierarchy in Africa', Journal des anthropologues, (142–3), pp. 29–47.

UN, G. and Ghana Statistical Service (2013) *Women & men in Ghana -2010 population and housing census report*. www.statsghana.gov.gh/docfiles/publica tions/2010phc_monograph_women_&_men_in_Gh.pdf (Accessed: 3 February 2014).

UNDP (2012) *Mobile Technologies and empowerment: Enhancing human development through participation and innovation*. www.undpegov.org/ sites/undpegov.org/files/undp_mobile_technology_primer.pdf (Accessed: 22 October 2013).

UNICEF, World Bank and WHO (2013) *Levels & trends in child mortality*. UN inter-agency group for child mortality estimation. www.childinfo.org/files/ Child_Mortality_Report_2013.pdf (Accessed: 12 May 2014).

Uteng, T. P. and Cresswell, T. (2008) *Gendered mobilities*. Aldershot: Ashgate. www.dawsonera.com/depp/reader/protected/external/AbstractView/ S9780754688990/S25.21/0 (Accessed: 26 January 2016).

Wade, R. H. (2002) 'Bridging the digital divide: New route to development or new form of dependency?', *Global Governance*, 8(4), pp. 443–66. https:// doi.org/10.2307/27800358.

Wajcman, J. (2000) 'Reflections on gender and technology studies: In what state is the art?', *Social Studies of Science*, 30(3), pp. 447–64, Published by: SAGE. [Preprint]. www.jstor.org/stable/285810.

Weil, O. *et al.* (2013) 'l'utilisation des nouvelles technologies de l'information et des communications (tic) dans le domaine de la sante maternelle et infantile en afrique subsaharienne'. www.afd.fr/webdav/site/afd/shared/ PUBLICATIONS/RECHERCHE/Scientifiques/Serie-grise/NTIC_sante.pdf (Accessed: 13 October 2016).

WHO (2011) *mHealth : New horizons for health through mobile technologies.*

WHO *et al.* (2012). *Trends in maternal mortality: 1990 to 2010 : WHO, UNICEF, UNFPA, and The World Bank estimates.* www.who.int/reproducti vehealth/publications/monitoring/9789241503631/en/ (Accessed: 12 May 2014).

WHO (2013) *World health statistics. 2013.* www.who.int/gho/publications/ world_health_statistics/EN_WHS2013_Part3.pdf?ua=1 (Accessed: 13 May 2014).

Wolf, J. A. *et al.* (2013) 'Diagnostic inaccuracy of smartphone applications for Melanoma detection', *JAMA Dermatology*, 149(4), p. 422. https://doi.org/ 10.1001/jamadermatol.2013.2382.

World Bank (2011) *Mobile applications for the health sector.* Washington, DC: World Bank. http://siteresources.worldbank.org/INFORMATIONAND COMMUNICATIONANDTECHNOLOGIES/Resources/mHealth_report_ (Apr_2012).pdf (Accessed: 20 December 2013).

World Bank (2012) *Maximizing mobile.* Washington, DC: World Bank : InfoDev (Information and communications for development, 2012).

Wyatt, S. (2005) 'The digital divide, health information and everyday life', *New Media & Society*, 7(2), pp. 199–218. https://doi.org/10.1177/146144480 5050747.

Wyatt, S. (2010) '« Les non-usagers de l'internet. Axes de recherche passés et futurs »', *Questions de communication [En ligne]*, (18). http://questionsde communication.revues.org/397.

Ya'u, Y. Z. (2004). 'The new imperialism & Africa in the global electronic village', *Review of African Political Economy*, 31(99), pp. 11–29.

Yu, Y., Li, J. and Liu, J. (2013) 'M-HELP: A miniaturized total health examin-ation system launched on a mobile phone platform', *Telemedicine Journal and e-health: The official journal of the American Telemedicine Association*, 19(11), pp. 857–865. doi:10.1089/tmj.2013.0031.

Yuval-Davis, N. (2015) 'Situated intersectionality and social inequality', *Raisons Politiques*, n58(2), pp. 75–89.

*To Mathieu, for being the most dedicated partner through all those years.*

Cambridge Elements ☰

# Global Development Studies

## Peter Ho
*Zhejiang University*

Peter Ho is Distinguished Professor at Zhejiang University and high-level National Expert of China. He has held or holds the position of, amongst others, Research Professor at the London School of Economics and Political Science and the School of Oriental and African Studies, Full Professor at Leiden University and Director of the Modern East Asia Research Centre, Full Professor at Groningen University and Director of the Centre for Development Studies. Ho is well-cited and published in leading journals of development, planning and area studies. He published numerous books, including with Cambridge University Press, Oxford University Press, and Wiley-Blackwell. Ho achieved the William Kapp Prize, China Rural Development Award and European Research Council Consolidator Grant. He chairs the International Conference on Agriculture and Rural Development (www.icardc.org) and sits on the boards of *Land Use Policy, Conservation and Society, China Rural Economics, Journal of Peasant Studies* and other journals.

## Servaas Storm
*Delft University of Technology*

Servaas Storm is a Dutch economist who has published widely on issues of macroeconomics, development, income distribution and economic growth, finance and climate change. He is Senior Lecturer at Delft University of Technology. He obtained a PhD in Economics (in 1992) from Erasmus University Rotterdam and worked as consultant for the ILO and UNCTAD. His latest book, co-authored with C. W. M. Naastepad, is *Macroeconomics Beyond the NAIRU* (Harvard University Press, 2012) and was awarded with the 2013 Myrdal Prize of the European Association for Evolutionary Political Economy. Servaas Storm is one of the editors of *Development and Change* (2006–now) and a member of the Institute for New Economic Thinking's Working Group on the Political Economy of Distribution.

## Advisory Board
Arun Agrawal, *University of Michigan*
Jun Borras, *International Institute of Social Studies*
Daniel Bromley, *University of Wisconsin-Madison*
Jane Carruthers, *University of South Africa*
You-tien Hsing, *University of California, Berkeley*
Tamara Jacka, *Australian National University*

## About the Series
The Cambridge Elements on Global Development Studies publishes ground-breaking, novel works that move beyond existing theories and methodologies of development in order to consider social change in real times and real spaces.

Cambridge Elements ≡

# Global Development Studies

Elements in the Series

*Temporary Migrants from Southeast Asia in Australia: Lost Opportunities*
Juliet Pietsch

*Mobile (for) Development: When Digital Giants Take Care of Poor Women*
Marine Al Dahdah

A full series listing is available at: www.cambridge.org/EGDS